Acknowledgements

To My Boss

I am dedicating this book, first of all, to my boss, my greatest mentor, my hero, my spiritual father and earthly dad, Jerry Savelle. He is the one who took a risk and a big step of faith positioning me as the Senior Vice President of his worldwide organization (with a *French* degree, I might add) for eleven years.

On day one as CEO, my dad said to me: "This organization is now entering Phase 2. In this phase we will work smarter, not harder, and accomplish more with less effort. Now, Terri, show us how we are going to do that."

Dad, your belief in me empowered me to believe more in myself. You gave me the opportunity to grow. You challenged me to solve problems, to implement vision, to develop myself, to grow others, and to force myself out of my comfort zone time and again.

It has been my greatest honor to serve as your CEO for Jerry Savelle Ministries International from 2003-2014. You are the greatest boss and

sweetest dad (and my favorite preacher) I could ever ask for! God truly transformed me into a leader. Because of this eleven-year experience, this book was written.

Thank you, Dad, for investing in my growth, trusting me with your ministry, believing in my calling, coaching me along the way, and loving me unconditionally.

> Leaders are made, they are not born; and they are made just like anything else has ever been made in this country – by hard work.
>
> — Vince Lombardi

To My Team

I also want to dedicate this leadership book to my amazing executive team who embraced the learning culture that I introduced. We discovered that leadership develops daily, not in a day. You traveled this journey with me week after week, year after year and transformed yourselves into effective leaders. You took ownership of your own personal growth. You loved the challenge and you provided wise counsel to help me make major

decisions.

You stood by my side, read every book with me page by page, attended numerous CEO workshops, seminars, and worked through countless hours of brainstorming sessions (while indulging in an array of various bundt cakes).

In essence, you made me look real smart!

Thank you for taking the challenge with me to never settle for being average, for stretching yourself, for becoming solution-minded, and for tapping into the leadership potential already within you.

Carolynn Rutan
Isaiah Shook
Carol Thurman
Donna Groover
Justin Bridges
Marty Manasco
Jesse Shook

Where no wise guidance is, the people fall, but in the multitude of counselors there is safety.

—Proverbs 11:14 AMP

The Leader's Checklist

10 action steps to inspire your team for success

978-1-942126-00-3

Published by Terri Savelle Foy Ministries
PO Box 1959
Rockwall, Tx 75087
www.terri.com

In association with The Fedd Agency, Inc.

Edited by A.J. Gregory and Layce Smith
Interior design by Layce Smith
Cover design by Micah Herrera

Printed in the United States of America
First Edition 2014

TERRI SAVELLE FOY

the LEADER'S CHECKLIST

10 action steps to inspire your team for success

selling author and my leadership mentor, John Maxwell, has made a lasting impression on my life. I remember reading that sentence for the first time and thinking, *Everything? Really? Everything rises and falls on MY ability to lead?* I wasn't completely convinced.

Maxwell's statement will either scare or inspire you. However, I believe it has the potential to do both. Fear of ruining a leadership opportunity might provide the discipline and drive that is necessary to succeed. In *Developing the Leader Within You* Maxwell shares a story that really illustrates this point.

> During a sales meeting, the manager was getting on to his staff about their dismally low sales figures. He said, "I have had just about enough of poor performance and excuses. If you can't do the job, perhaps there are other sales people out there who would jump at the chance to sell the worthy products that each of you has the privilege to represent."
>
> Then pointing to a new recruited, retired pro-football player, he said, "Hey, if a

football team isn't winning, what happens? The players are replaced, right?" The question hung heavy for a few seconds, then the ex-football player answered, "Actually sir, if the whole team is having trouble, we usually got a new coach."

This story woke me up to the hard truth: Everything—from productivity, customer satisfaction, and net profit, down to the morale of company employees and the cleanliness of our facilities —does, in fact, rise and fall on my ability to lead. There is a lot at stake!

In *The 21 Irrefutable Laws of Leadership* (which I highly recommend you read) Maxwell shares another story of meeting Don Stevenson, the chairman of Global Hospitality Resources of San Diego, California, an international hospitality and advisory consultant firm.

Over lunch, I asked him about his organization. Today, he primarily does consulting but back then, his company took over the management of hotels and resorts that weren't doing well financially. They oversaw many excellent facilities such as La Costa in Southern California. Don said that whenever they came into an organization to take it over, they always started by doing two things: First, they trained all the staff to improve their level of service to the customer and second, they fired the leader.

Maxwell continues: "When he told me that, I was at first surprised."

"You always fire him?" I asked. "Every time?"
"That's right. Every time." He said.
"Don't you talk to the person first to check him out, see if he's really a good leader?" I said.
"No," he said, "If he'd been a good leader, the organization wouldn't be in the mess it's in."[1]

Don't throw in the towel just yet! Let that story encourage you to embark on a quest toward

---

[1] John Maxwell, The 21 Irrefutable Laws of Leadership (Thomas Nelson, 2007), page 8-9.

successful leadership. Luckily, getting rid of an existing leader isn't the only way to see change. Like me, you can learn and grow into a great leader. I am the poster child of hope that you can develop into a good leader.

T.D. Jakes once said, "If you have a pastor who has the capacity to lead 100 people and you give him a church of 1,000 people, he will lose 900 people. However, if you have a pastor who has the capacity to lead 1,000 people and you give him 100 people, he will gain 900 people." Everything will be determined by your quality of leadership.

Let's cover some basics: What is leadership? According to the U.S. Army, "Leadership is influencing people—by providing purpose, direction, and motivation—while operating to accomplish the mission and improve the organization."

Sounds like a great deal of responsibility, doesn't it? Well, it is. And it doesn't sound like something that happens overnight. It sounds like a growth process, and the purpose of this book is to help you through that process.

Within *The Leader's Checklist* you will find ten simple, practical, and effective action steps I've taken to develop my leadership abilities.

Whether you lead a company, a church, a network marketing team, a youth group, a department, or a home, the information I share will benefit you and help you reach the next level.

This list came about after a meeting I had with a dear friend whose husband had died of a sudden heart attack. She and her late husband had been in ministry together for over twenty years, pastoring a 2,000-member church, establishing Bible schools, supporting orphanages, and assisting widows. Her husband was a strong, confident leader and had managed the organization well since its conception. After his death, she became the sole leader of everything.

This woman called me one day and said, "Terri, I don't even know where to start! I'm so overwhelmed. I'm totally different from my husband. I don't lead the way he led. Is there anything you can tell me that would help me lead this organization to see it thrive and not fall apart?" I told her I would think about it and get back to her in a few days.

As I reflected on what made me an effective leader, I came up with ten steps I have practiced consistently for over eleven years in order to see significant growth in our organization, worldwide influence through TV broadcasts, book distribution, and online media, and tremendous financial stability.

If you have recently stepped into a leadership role and feel insecure or unsure, then this book is for you. This book is also for you if you have been in leadership for a while but feel stuck. Finally, this book is for you if you strive to be a great leader one day.

It is my prayer that whatever your journey into leadership looks like, you embrace the process of growth and develop into the leader God has called you to be.

> To change the direction of the
> organization, change the leader.
> —John Maxwell

Chapter One

1

Develop a Plan for Personal Growth

> Success is something you attract by the
> person you become.
> —Jim Rohn

First things first, don't even think about becoming the best *leader* you can be without planning how to become the best *you* that you can be. I've heard Jim Rohn say, "Success is something you attract by the person you become." In other words, if you want more, you must become more.

Ten months prior to becoming the CEO of Jerry Savelle Ministries, I began practicing some daily disciplines for personal growth. These practices had a profound impact on my self-esteem, my health, my profession, and my relationship with God. Little did I know that these key behaviors were preparing me for the leadership position I would be given.

I had no strategic plan outlined for me by a professional life coach; it was something I created on my own and determined to practice each day for twenty-one days without interruption. After twenty-two days, I didn't want to stop. So, I continued for another month. Then, at the end of that thirty-day time frame, I kept going. That was in 2002, and I haven't stopped.

My plan was simple. I would commit to do the following every day:

1. pray
2. listen to a motivational message
3. read from a motivational book
4. review my list of dreams and goals
5. exercise

At the launch of these disciplines, I was desperate for direction in my life, hope for my future, and vision to do something—anything! I had no idea the impact five simple practices would have on my life and, consequently, the lives of others. "Personal growth" was a term I was unfamiliar with. (I had never even heard of Jim Rohn for that matter.) I just wanted change! Well, that simple little plan returned huge dividends. You can't argue with results; and I like the results, so I will keep the plan.

Below are the particulars. You may want to consider adopting some of these practices as your own.

Pray

I said to myself that every day I would do something to invest in my relationship with God, whether it was for five minutes, twenty minutes, or an hour.

I began to pray. Not only that, I began listening to hear God's voice. Also, I journaled my time with Him, which led to receiving direction for my life and, later, for our organization. This daily time spent in prayer altered the course of my direction. And it continues to do so!

Listen

Each day, I listened to a motivational message. I had to ask myself, "*What* will I listen to?" I obtained talks from speakers including Joyce Meyer, Jerry Savelle, John Maxwell, Mac Hammond, and others that inspired, motivated, and challenged me in order to grow more.

Next, I had to ask myself, "*When* will I listen?"

I had to be realistic about how I would be *consistent* with this new discipline.

I concluded that the morning hours of getting dressed and preparing for my day would be the best time for me to implement and stick with this new habit. I have to get ready anyway, so why not use that time to invest in myself rather than fill my mind with useless talk radio or music that doesn't prepare me for my future?

I placed an audio device in the bathroom, pushed play every morning, and listened to uplifting messages while getting ready.

This simple habit challenged me to think bigger, dream higher, and believe for greater things in my life. What you repeatedly hear, you will eventually believe. Romans 10:17 says faith comes by hearing. I can't help but have great faith when I hear the Word every single day. And when I use my time to get ready in the morning as a time to fill my mind with positive messages, then very little effort is required for my growth.

Read

Perhaps you've heard "leaders are readers." I set a goal to read for twenty minutes each day. I admit, in the beginning, it was a chore. I never enjoyed the pleasures of reading. The only books I ever read (aside from school requirements) were *The Dallas Cowboys Cheerleaders Manual* and the life story of gymnast Mary Lou Retton! Needless to say, I forced myself to develop this discipline by literally setting the timer on my phone for twenty minutes and focusing as best as I could.

Over time, I absorbed such life-changing information that I didn't want to stop when the alarm sounded. I read for thirty minutes, sometimes a full hour. This practice has increased my desire to read. Now, I love it! Doing this has taught me that you can change your desires by changing what you give attention to. As you focus more and more on a new discipline, your desires change with it.

Review

> For as he thinks in his heart, so is he.
> —Proverbs 23:7 AMP

What you think about, you bring about. Not a day goes by that I don't review my dreams and goals. I

»→Begin a dream & goals journal.

6

used to journal goals like: eliminate debt of $3,000; clean the kitchen; wash the car; finish reading the book. However, as my thinking grew, my dreams and goals grew. For example, "finish reading the book" eventually became "finish *writing* the book." "Wash the car" became "pay cash for the car."

As I began reviewing my dreams daily, my desire to see them achieved escalated. I became more diligent and determined in the pursuit of my dreams because they were constantly before my eyes. Consequently, everything I would write down began happening. They happened because there is a spiritual law that reveals whatever you keep before your eyes will eventually show up in your life.

*Note: You can access our Dreams and Goals application for your iPhone and iPad in the iTunes App Store.

Exercise

I committed to doing some kind of physical activity every day. Initially, I began this discipline by saying, "I will walk for 20 minutes in my neighborhood for the next 21 days." At the end of

21 days, I didn't want to stop this habit, because I felt so much better inside and out. I also liked being described as "disciplined" and "committed." I increased my exercise from twenty minutes to thirty minutes until I climbed up to an hour a day. To this day, I haven't stopped.

Why Growth Matters

A plan for personal growth fosters an outlook on life that says, "If it is to be, it's up to me." It is taking full responsibility for the direction of your life and the results that follow. To begin down this path, I want you to identify the dreams, goals, and aspirations of your personal growth and the key competencies that will have the greatest impact on your life.

In essence, you need to develop a plan to become better. Many adults think that growth is automatic and will continue without effort; however, without strategic steps to grow, you will stagnate. When you stop growing, you stop. I'll never forget the day I graduated from college. With the end of my classes, I declared that I would never study again. It was the dumbest thing I have ever said. However, my declaration was backed up by action for many years, resulting in a life of little progress.

We want better things—a better job, a better salary, a better marriage, a better body, a better career, better opportunities, better profit margins, better staff, etc.—not realizing the only way to *have* better is to *become* better. By the end of this chapter, you will have an opportunity to outline a practical, intentional plan for growth that will impact your life and your organization. My hope is that you stick to it!

It wasn't until 2002 that my unhealthy habits of complacency and stagnation changed by implementing this plan for growth. It occurred after I heard John Maxwell on *Today Matters* make a very bold claim.

> If I could come to your house and spend just one day with you, I would be able to tell whether or not you will be successful. You could pick the day. Let me watch you from the moment you wake up until you go to bed that night. Just by observing you in one 24-hour period, I could tell in what direction your life is headed.

Why would he make such a bold statement? As I continued to listen out of curiosity, he said, "Many times I make that statement at conferences and people get a little upset with me and they think my claim sounds arrogant." He explained, "Here's why I say that: The secret of your future is revealed in your daily agenda. If you want to see change in your life, change something you do daily."

Today when people ask how I know so many motivational phrases and quotes, I tell them it's because I listen to a motivational message every day. When people ask how I'm able to speak confidently to thousands of people, I tell them I declare confidence in my prayer time to speak to thousands of people.

How do you have the energy to fly overseas, speak in conferences, and not suffer from jet lag?
By exercising every day, I have more energy.

Why is it that you seem to attain all of your dreams and goals?
Every day I review my list of dreams and goals, and whatever you keep before your eyes will eventually show up in your life.

You get the point. Focusing on personal growth and committing to daily disciplines influenced change in my life and in my future. When you decide to improve yourself through a personal growth plan, conditions around you will begin to improve.

John Maxwell shared in his book, *The 15 Invaluable Laws of Growth,* a story of meeting a gentleman named Kirk Campmeier in the early 1970s. Campmeier asked Maxwell about his plan for personal growth.

When he began listing all of his accomplishments and his goals for that year, Campmeier stopped him and said, "No, John, what is your plan for personal growth?" Thinking about it, he replied, "I guess I really don't have a plan for personal growth." Campmeier was selling a growth kit for $799. Maxwell could not afford the kit, but he knew it would give him a strategic and intentional plan for growth. (You have to realize that growth is not a period of life; it is a way of life.)

Well, Maxwell talked to his wife, Margaret. They didn't have extra money to spend on a growth kit, so they skipped lunches, passed on the family vacation, and did without some things until they had enough to buy the kit.

In the meantime, John began asking everyone he knew if they had a plan for personal growth and what that plan was. He said not one person in his world had a plan to grow. Thus, no one in his world was growing.

John bought that kit and now claims, "Next to my faith, this has been the greatest decision in my life, a plan to grow, a decision to grow."

Can you imagine taking your biggest financial challenge to someone like Donald Trump? He would probably laugh that you even think it's a financial challenge. He would laugh at my financial challenges. Why is that? Because of who he has become. The size of the challenge depends on the size of the person, so the key is to become bigger than your challenges. This occurs overtime as you continue to grow, educate yourself, and embark on a daily journey of learning.

Another mentor of mine, Pastor Joel Sims of Jackson, Mississippi, shared a similar story of how he began developing himself. When he was an 18-year-old senior in high school, getting ready for college, he felt like he had the world at his feet. However, with one knock on the door of his math class, Joel knew his life was about to change.

When he was called out of class that day, Joel was told his father had suddenly died of a massive heart attack. His dad was there at breakfast, and he wasn't there for dinner. Joel's whole world changed in one instant.

After graduation, Joel went to Bible college. His dad had pastored a church for over twenty years, so Joel thought he needed to go to Bible school to help his mom pastor the church her husband had built.

During his first year of college, Joel felt in his heart that he needed to be back home helping his mom run the church. So, he flew back to Jackson, Mississippi, and began pastoring his dad's church at 19 years old. Well, in the first year of pastoring the church, he lost more than half the crowd (half the crowd means half the income). He realized something needed to change or he would lose everything that his dad had spent twenty years building.

Joel was desperate. He began removing every distraction in his life. He took all the TVs out of his house and bought some CDs and books on everything from personal growth to leadership,

>>> Remove distractions, add books & CDs on personal growth & leadership.

13

finances, relationships and spiritual growth. He set a goal to listen to two CDs a day and read one book a week. (That is fifty-two books in a year; that's desperate.)

Joel also began to watch other people. He said, "I would watch Joel Osteen, how he used body language while he was ministering to make a point. I would watch John Maxwell, how he would just sit calmly during his entire speech. When he really wanted to get the point across, he would stand up. I watched T.D. Jakes, how he used voice inflection to stress a point."

Well, he committed to this plan for personal growth. That was ten years ago. He's now 29 years old. He pastors over 3,000 people. He just paid off the mortgage on his church, a brand new building worth 11.5 million dollars. How did he meet such success? He was on a quest for personal growth. He developed a plan to change himself and his whole world began to change with it.

The Bible says to whom much is given, much is required.[1] Well, God has called you to be a leader. Some people are with you only for a season—

---

1 Luke 12:48 (English Standard Version).

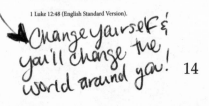
Change yourself &
you'll change the
world around you!

14

employees, volunteers, or coworkers—so think about what you want them to say about your leadership. What do you want them to say about how you coached them?

Do you want them to say, "I learned so much when I was working with him," or, "I learned so much under her leadership"? You can't just pray to be a good leader and suddenly gain respect any more than you can just pray to speak French and automatically become fluent. You have to study, and the motivation to do so begins with a daily routine.

(handwritten margin note: Great point about leadership & respect.)

The Secret to Your Future is in Your Daily Routine

I am thoroughly convinced that the secret of your future is hidden in your daily routine. When activities are performed at the same time each day, they tend to become automatic. Leaving my house or hotel room in the morning without reviewing my dreams and goals would feel strange because I have committed to this discipline each morning for years. It's now a part of my daily routine. It would almost feel like leaving the house without applying makeup—and that would never happen!

Joyce Meyer asked a man who had been in ministry for over forty years what would be one thing that could keep her ministry from falling into temptation and failing. The elderly man thought about it for a moment and then said, "Whatever you did to get to where you're at, DON'T STOP DOING IT!"[2]

When my daily routine changed, my life changed. I began to realize that one massive three-hour workout will not help me lose weight; walking twenty minutes each day, however, will bring change in my health. It's not one entire morning of prayer that will change my circumstances; it's through daily conversations with God (about everything) that brings about change. It's not depositing one paycheck into my savings account that prepares me for my financial future; it is a portion of every paycheck going into my savings account that changes my life. It's what you do on a daily basis that leads you closer to your dreams or further from them. Change your routine; change your life.

---

2 Joyce Meyer, Closing the Door to Satanic Attack CD, Joyce Meyer Ministries.

Basketball legend, Larry Bird, used to shoot 500 free throw shots a day. You've probably heard "Champions don't become champions in the ring; they are merely recognized there." If you want to see how someone develops into a champion, look at their daily routine. Observe, like Maxwell says, how they utilize their time.

What if you set a goal to read for twenty minutes a day? It's not a lot of time, is it? You can surely find twenty minutes in your day to commit to personal growth. It may not sound like much, but twenty minutes a day is ten hours a month. That's a good chunk of time! And that's how I got started.

Successful People = Successful Habits

New York Times best-selling author, Debbie Macomber, has published more than 150 books, many of them best sellers turned made-for-television movies. Over 170 million copies of her books are in print, and she has millions of loyal fans. She also has a "dream routine."

Every day, Debbie wakes up at 4:30 a.m., reads her Bible, and writes in her journal. By 6:00 a.m.

she is swimming laps in her pool. At 7:30 a.m. she answers her mail in her office. From 10:00 a.m. to 4:00 p.m., she writes. The result of Debbie's routine is that she produces an average of three new books a year.

The secret of your future is hidden in your daily routine. If you change your routine, you can change your life.

Forbes Magazine published an article titled, "5 things successful people do before 8:00 a.m.," which researched how successful people utilize their morning hours. They recognized a common trait of "early rising" in many CEOs, government officials, and other people of influence.

According to *Inc. Magazine*, morning people are generally more proactive and more productive.

- Margaret Thatcher was up every day at 5 a.m.
- Frank Lloyd Wright at 4 a.m.
- Robert Iger, the CEO of Disney wakes up at 4:30 a.m.

Let's explore five things successful people do before eight o'clock.

1. Exercise.
Most people who work out daily do it in the morning. The morning hours seem to be when we have the most control over our time. Of course, the best way to start a habit is to do it at the same time each day. If you work better at night, by all means, work as a night owl.

2. Map Out Your Day.
Successful people maximize their potential by having a well-thought-out schedule for the day as well as daily goals and to-do lists. I never go to bed without planning the next day.

3. Eat a Healthy Breakfast.
Only in recent years did I discover that breakfast actually means "break the fast." Your body has been fasting for the six to eight hours you've been sleeping, and the fast needs to be broken to replenish your energy. Never skip breakfast, especially if you're trying to lose weight. You need the energy and healthy nutrients as you begin your day.

4. Visualize.

Jack Nicklaus, the legendary golfer, once said, "I never hit a shot, not even in practice, without having a very sharp, in-focus picture of it in my head first." He understood the importance of visualizing success before you step out.

Many experts recommend utilizing the morning hours to visualize. Harvard University researched students who visualized their tasks prior to performing them and found that they had nearly a 100 percent success rate when it came to the actual fulfillment of that task. Students who did not visualize had about a 55 percent rate of achievement.

I recommend visualizing, or seeing with your eye of faith, your dreams and goals accomplished. Let your faith rise as you "act as if" it's already happened. Remember, faith sees what other people can't see.

The morning is the perfect time to allocate quiet time inside your mind, meditating or visualizing. Take a moment to visualize the day ahead of you, focusing on the successes you will have. Every morning, I spend time alone before heading off to work, praying over my dreams and goals.

5. Make Your Day Top Heavy.

We all have that one item on our to do list that we dread, whether that's budget planning, sending follow-up emails, performing damage control, or leading a staff meeting. It looms over us all day (or week) until we finally suck it up and get it done.

Rather than continuing to put off that project until a more convenient time, put it at the top of your list. Everything else will seem minute compared to completing this task. You will go to sleep feeling satisfied because the most important assignment was finished.

The Rule of 5

John Maxwell has coined the phrase "The rule of 5," which describes a series of five activities you practice every day that become fundamental to success. Maxwell personally practices the following five daily disciplines every day: (1) he reads, (2) he files, (3) he thinks, (4) he asks questions, and (5) he writes. John Maxwell, adamantly claims that his "rule of 5" has been paramount to his success.

Honestly, my personal "rule of 5" only takes

up about 15-20% of my entire day. I am finished with all five by eight o'clock in the morning. Trust me, you may think you are too busy to stick with these five things, but you can't afford not to invest in this time.

Establish Your Dream Routine

> Devoting a little of yourself to everything means committing a great deal of yourself to nothing.
> – Michael LeBoef

We make time for what's most important to us. Extraordinary leaders are developed in their daily routine. As you think about your most important goals and dreams to accomplish, there will be strategic action steps that you should take each day to move you closer.

- These steps are unique to your dreams and goals.
- These steps become ingrained in your daily life.
- These steps, when practiced over time, will

set you apart from your competition or others in your field.
- These steps are deliberate and intentional.
- These steps improve your performance, your confidence, and your results.

What are *your* five? What action steps can you incorporate in your daily routine to catapult you into a successful future?

Take some time and think about these things. Think of the possibilities. Think of what you can accomplish with the right disciplines and daily routine. Write them down in the space below.

_____

_____

_____

God has too much planned for your life for you to stay where you are. Pablo Casals started playing the cello at the age of twelve and became known around the world as the best in his field. At 85 years old, he still got up every morning and practiced five hours a day. When a reporter asked why he put in so much effort Pablo smiled and said, "I think I'm getting better." Never stop investing in yourself.

Joel Osteen said, "If your skill level hasn't changed in the past five years, then you are at a major disadvantage. Others are growing all around you. Others will be promoted. Why not you?"

> Do you see a man skilled in their work?
> They will stand before kings and great
> men.
> —Proverbs 22:29

Never stop growing, learning, developing, attending educational conferences, going to training seminars, reading books, listening to audio messages, and committing yourself to a strategic, intentional plan for growth.

Chapter Two

2

Obtain the Vision

The very essence of leadership is that you
have to have vision. You can't blow an
uncertain trumpet.
                    – Theodore M. Hesburgh

Do you know any successful person without an
idea of the direction they want to go? Me neither!
As a leader, vision is the vital organ keeping your
organization, your team, or your department
alive.

Vision is the sight of the mind. It is your
imagination working to envision your future.
Proverbs 29:18 says, "Where there is no vision,
the people perish." What your team wants more
than anything from you is direction. They want to
know where they're headed.

Where there is no vision for the company, the
company will perish. Where there's no vision for
the church, the church will perish. Where there
is no vision for the marriage, the marriage will

perish. This is true in every area of life. Vision keeps you alive. It takes you from where you are to where you want to be. As Rick Warren says:

> "If you want to know the temperature of your organization, put a thermometer in the leader's mouth. Leaders can never take their people farther than they have traveled. Therefore, the focus of vision must be on the leader—like leader, like people. Followers find the leader and then the vision. Leaders find the vision and then the people."

Put Your Dream to the Test

> Beds all over the world are full of dreamers,
> but not people with vision.
> —Unknown

I read a story about a little Australian boy named Peter. His parents were third generation welfare recipients, and he suffered from a learning disability. He was misunderstood by his teacher and told he was a bad boy who would never amount to anything. Consequently, he failed every grade in school.

As an adult, Peter went into business for himself on three separate occasions, failing and going broke each time. But he wouldn't give up. Today Peter Daniels is a famed author, life coach, and speaker recognized for many successful ventures in various countries across the globe. His confidants and closest friends include royalty, heads of state, and many of the most successful entrepreneurs of our time. A charitable man, Daniels uses a significant portion of his multi-million-dollar portfolio to invest in philanthropic efforts.

When asked how he turned his failures into unprecedented success, Peter replied, "I scheduled time to think. In fact, I reserve one day a week on my calendar just to think. All of my greatest ideas, opportunities, and money-making ventures started with the days I took off to think."[3]

This is where most people miss the mark; they don't think. They rarely ever schedule time to stop the busyness of life and just meditate, ponder,

3 Jack Canfield, Mark Victor Hansen, & Les Hewitt, The Power of Focus (Vintage/Ebury, 2011).

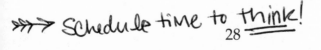
Schedule time to think!

envision, or dream. Think about your future. Think about the next five years. Think about the changes you want to see in your organization, your church, or your family.

Like Peter, John Maxwell knows that "thinking precedes achievement. Nobody just stumbles upon success and then tries to figure it out afterwards." The greater your thinking, the greater your potential. Get away with God and just think, imagine, and give yourself permission to dream. Let God speak to you. Ask Him, "What is the vision you want me to pursue? What do you want to see accomplished?"

Trying to make something work without vision is like trying to assemble a 1,000-piece puzzle without a picture on the box top. Having a bag full of puzzle pieces doesn't guarantee you'll be able to put it together. You don't know if the puzzle is a piano. You don't know if it's the Empire State Building. You don't know if it's a giant cupcake. You have no idea what this puzzle is meant to depict—you just know you need to put it together.

After a while you're going to get bored. You're going to get frustrated. You're not even going to want to get up in the morning, because you don't know what you're doing. But as soon as someone gives you the picture—*Oh, it's the Eiffel Tower!*—it all of a sudden makes sense. You know what you're doing. You know what you're trying to accomplish and you have motivation to finish. That's what happens when you get vision for your life, organization, your ministry, or your church.

If you do not have a picture in your mind of what you want to do with your life, then you're just busy. You're killing time and throwing away your own potential. That is not God's best for your life.

How to Find Your Vision

> The most pathetic person in the world is someone who has sight, but has no vision.
> —Helen Keller

Warren Buffett's "5-Step Process for Prioritizing True Success" from *Forbes Magazine* discusses ways to find your vision. Buffett is recognized as one of the most influential people in the world today, so it might be helpful to absorb his list.

1. Know what you want – List your top 25.

Years ago, it was reported that Warren Buffet approached his pilot and said, "You should be going after more of your goals and dreams." Warren then asked him to list the top 25 things he wanted to do in the next few years or his lifetime. He challenged him to write down anything important to him that wasn't currently a part of his life.

It's interesting how, as a baby, you knew what you wanted. You knew when you were hungry. You knew which foods you enjoyed. And you made it pretty clear which foods you didn't by spitting them out without reservation. You had no trouble expressing your wants.

So what happened? You grew up and discovered (or you were told):

- You can't have everything you want because you want it.
- Money doesn't grow on trees.
- You're so selfish. Life isn't all about what you want.

The result: YOU STOP THINKING ABOUT WHAT YOU WANT.

In order to discover your vision, you must figure out what you want. This concept seems so simple, but most people have no idea what they want.

Brian Tracy says, "Clarity is the most important single quality of goal-setting and perhaps the most important single quality of success." Vague goals produce vague results. Nobody wants to rally behind a blurred vision. Be specific.

- Save $10,000 by December 31.
- Launch our television broadcast by September 30.
- Eliminate debts of $18,000 by March 31.
- Purchase our new facility by June 1.
- Mentor 1,000 people by August 1.

You must know what you want before you can communicate a compelling vision for others to support. Let me point out the importance of writing our goals. First of all, God said to do it. This is a success trait practiced by the most influential people in the world, but many do not realize that it was God's idea. This principle originated all the way back in Habakkuk 2:2: "Write the vision and make it plain upon tablets."

Through the years, people have stumbled upon this skill and attained amazing results. Andrew Carnegie, the steel magnate, hired a young Napoleon Hill to do research for him on successful people. He asked Napoleon to interview 500 of the wealthiest people at the time to discover what made them so successful. He was searching for a common trait among these millionaires that could help others become wealthy.

Napoleon interviewed people like Thomas Edison, Henry Ford, Theodore Roosevelt, John D Rockefeller, John Wannamaker, Charles Schwabb, and many more. He went back to Andrew Carnegie with the astounding results that they did, in fact, have a common success trait. Each one admitted to having clearly defined, written goals!

Statistics show that only three percent of living Americans, or adults anywhere for that matter, have written goals. However, they are the most successful!

Brian Tracy said that as a leader, success begins with a pad of paper, a pen, and a few minutes of your time. All successful people have the habit of thinking on paper. If you cannot write your vision (your dreams or goals) clearly on a piece of paper, then you have not thought it through yet.

I don't even know how to explain it, but something amazing happens when you actually write a goal down. It's been described as the equivalent of programming your GPS and suddenly knowing where to drive. You are literally programming directions for your life into your subconscious mind. By writing down your vision, your desire to see the goal accomplished elevates. It's a proven fact that if you aim at nothing, you'll hit it every time.

2. Pick your Top 5.

Once Warren's pilot completed his list of twenty-five things, Warren asked him to review each item and circle the top five that he wanted more than anything. At first, the pilot was reluctant because they all seemed pretty important to him, but Warren insisted on picking only five. What are the TOP 5 dreams and goals you wrote down in the first chapter? Focus on these things.

3. Make your Top 5 Plan.

After narrowing his list to five items, Buffet asked his pilot when he would work on his goals. Never set a goal without establishing when you plan to go after it. Based on my experience, if you do not schedule a specific time in which you will pursue this dream, it will NEVER happen.

Look at your calendar and realistically appoint a time to make it happen. It's always comforting to tell ourselves we'll start something tomorrow, but that's only an excuse and a way of procrastinating.

> Tomorrow is the only day of the year that appeals to a lazy man.
> —Jimmy Lyons

Set a deadline. Deadlines are motivating! *SO True!*
The best motivation for cleaning your house is inviting company over. Suddenly, the clutter you have been putting off clearing gets organized in no time! Why? There's a deadline!

- Set a deadline on your savings goal.
- Set a deadline on getting life insurance.

- Set a deadline on finishing the mission statement.
- Set a deadline on paying off that loan.
- Set a deadline on opening your new account.
- Set a deadline on developing that new employee.
- Set a deadline on getting your degree.
- Set a deadline on enrolling in those classes.
- Set a deadline on finding your core team members.
- Set a deadline on launching that new division.
- Set a deadline on opening your business.

What happens if I set a goal and I don't achieve it by the deadline?

The answer is simple: Set another deadline.

4. Marry your priorities.

According to Warren Buffet, you must be committed to your top five goals. When he asked his pilot about the twenty items not circled on the list, the pilot said he would work on them intermittently as he worked through the five. Warren replied, "You've got it wrong....Everything you didn't circle just became your 'avoid at all cost list.' No matter what, these things get no attention from you until you've succeeded with your top 5."[4]

> Perhaps the two most important qualities
> of success are focus and concentration.
> —Brian Tracy

Focus is identifying exactly what you want. Concentration is the ability and the discipline to focus on one thing, the most important thing, until it is complete. Finish the task at hand. Don't move on to a new priority until the first one is complete.

5. Know your "Avoid at all Cost" list and stick to it.

Most people try to focus on too many things and end up not accomplishing any of them. Big dreams happen when we are not distracted by other pursuits. That's why it is so important to focus on your top five and ignore the rest.

Take Warren's advice and begin listing your goals. Do you want to grow your organization? Do you want to implement new products? Do

---

4 Scott Dinsmore, Warren Buffett's 5-Step Process for Prioritizing True Success (and Why Most People Never Do It), Live Your Legend, February, 1, 2011, (http://liveyourlegend.net/warren-buffetts-5-step-process-for-prioritizing-true-success-and-why-most-people-never-do-it/).

you want to expand your services? Do you want to create a spirit of community and teamwork? What do you feel you need to accomplish to fulfill your assignment? Your team is waiting to hear this clarity of direction from you.

Imagine to Find Your Vision

> One must realize that all who have accumulated great fortunes first did a certain amount of dreaming, hoping, wishing, desiring and planning before they acquired money.
>
> —Napoleon Hill

I've been told the African impala has the ability to jump ten feet high and thirty feet long. At the same time, you will find this little animal trapped behind a four-foot wall at the zoo, not even attempting to get out. Why? Because the impala has to "see" where he's headed before he'll take a step toward it. He cannot see over the wall; therefore, he stays confined.

You will also stay confined year after year— even though you have the potential to go far—

without a mental picture of where you're headed. See beyond the four-foot wall you've lingered behind for far too long. God sees your potential; now you need to. Don't limit yourself and remain trapped in complacency when you have the ability to go much further.

You will never leave where you are until you see in your mind where you'd rather be. Picture yourself doing something that seems impossible or out of reach. Once you are able to imagine it, you are one step closer to having it. If you can't imagine success in your mind, or in your heart, you'll never have it in your hands.

> Everybody ends up somewhere in life;
> a few people end up somewhere on
> purpose. Those are the ones with vision.
> —Andy Stanley

For years, my life was stagnant and lacked change in any area. My weight stayed the same, my debt stayed the same, my savings account stayed the same, my marriage, my self-image, my home life—everything stayed the same. Each year was a repeat of the year before. I existed, but I was not doing much of anything. Sure, I could stay busy, but I was not succeeding in my purpose.

I heard people teach about "writing your vision and dreams on paper," and I would get excited. However, I still lacked vision and direction.

Finally, I gave myself permission to dream. Imagine. Think big. I sat in my guest bedroom with nothing but a laptop and my imagination. I began to imagine life five years into the future. *What do I see myself doing?* Whatever came across my mind, I wrote it down. I was not 100 percent sure that what I "saw" in my imagination was God's perfect will for my life, but I wrote it down anyway. The dreams I wrote were so big and audacious! I had no idea if they could actually be attained.

Interestingly enough, every single thing I wrote down happened. That's the power of a written vision.

Doubt is one of the biggest obstacles to your success. If you immediately start asking the "How?" questions, you will stop any progress before it starts. I want you to realize that this applies to your organizational team as well. You need everyone operating in faith and expectancy.

It will be very difficult to move forward if doubt is the controlling force.

How in the world will we ever create this new program?
How will we ever host our own conference with thousands of people?
How will I we ever break that revenue barrier?
How will we ever get our books in bookstores around the world?
How will we ever help that many people each month?
How will we ever increase our sales by 50%?
How will we ever buy land and build our own building?
How will we ever operate debt-free?

As the leader, focus on what your mind can imagine, not how you will obtain it. Getting stuck on the "how" will only derail you from dreaming big. Teach your team to not put limits on themselves and God's ability to open their minds to great things. The more time invested in imagining the future, the more ideas God will give you.

Make a decision right now that you will give yourself permission to dream and dream big! Without any concern about how it will come to pass, what can you imagine? *That* is what God wants you to see!

> Find out what it is you want and go after
> it as if your life depends on it. Why?
> Because it does.
> —Les Brown

I want to challenge you to obtain the vision. Sit quietly with God and just think. Write down whatever comes to mind, even if you're not sure whether it's God or if you're making it up.

Your job as a leader is to never take your eyes off the vision. In *Developing the Leader Within You*, John Maxwell describes "4 Vision levels of People":

1. Some people never see it. (They are wanderers.)
2. Some people see it but never pursue it on their own. (They are followers.)
3. Some people see it and pursue it. (They are achievers.)
4. Some people see it and pursue it and help others see it. (They are leaders.)

Whether you've been in business or ministry for over thirty years or you are just starting out, sometimes you have to go back and refine your vision. See where you're at, assess your passion, and discover what God wants you to accomplish. Remember, God's vision for your life is much bigger than you.

Chapter Three

3

Build Your Dream Team

It takes teamwork to make the dream
work.
—John Maxwell

Vision is something that comes from you, the
leader. The steps to achieve the vision come from
your team, the people who God has brought to
help you fulfill the vision. You can only achieve
your dreams with the help of others.

Allow me to utilize my French degree by
describing teamwork with an expression the
French use: *esprit de corps.* This means a sense
of unity, enthusiasm for common interests and
responsibilities, devotion for a cause, or strong
regard for the honor of the group.

Teams rise to a new level when they come
together to accomplish a common goal. Working
with a team, as a team, not only benefits the
members but *significantly* affects your business or
organization as a whole.

> No man will make a great leader who
> wants to do it all himself or to get all the
> credit for doing it.
> —Andrew Carnegie

This concept may be new or a bit challenging to adopt, especially if you are accustomed to working alone. This principle of working as a team was hammered repeatedly during the first CEO workshop I attended. Dr. Dean Radtke, founder & CEO of The Institute of Ministry Management & Leadership and my personal mentor, exclaimed, "Nobody works alone!"

Successful leaders do not act solely as individuals. The role of a leader is to guide those under them to find solutions that work best collectively. Effective leaders bring people together not with a sense of superiority but with a sense of unity for a common vision.

Others Around You Matter

> Coming together is a beginning. Keeping
> together is progress. Working together is
> success.
> —Henry Ford

After twelve hours of CEO training, I knew my first directive was to build a team. I understood completely that teamwork is essential. (Even the *Lone* Ranger wasn't alone; everywhere he went, Tonto was right there with him.) Working with a team creates synergy where the sum is greater than the parts. People feel empowered to tap into their strengths in an effort to bring something new to the table. It promotes a sense of achievement, which is vital to a positive environment.

When your team works well together, the company benefits, as a whole, benefits. When I began adapting this new mode of operation in our organization, I can attest that communication improved, morale increased, and results compounded.

Here are five benefits of working as a team:

1. Efficiency

As team members communicate regularly through scheduled meetings, you will improve efficiency. When everyone on the team knows what tasks, events, and projects the other members are working on, it eliminates the last-minute emergencies, unplanned budgeting, and unnecessary stress.

Innovation

Creativity skyrockets when a team comes together to brainstorm ideas. It's invigorating to watch a group of extremely different people with varied backgrounds, interests, experiences, and personalities collaborate. One thought, one idea leads to another, which could lead to the winning solution for the team that year.

2. Enthusiasm

Passion and excitement spread when teams meet regularly to work toward common goals. When employees go great lengths of time without any corporate gathering, except for the annual spring picnic and the yearly Christmas karaoke party, morale plummets.

3. Financial Stability

With consistent communication among teams there are no surprises in the monthly budgets. Projects and events are planned in advance, money is allocated accordingly, and stress is consequently reduced.

4. Unity

The phrase "all for one and one for all" accompanies teamwork. You literally become a close-knit family when you stay involved in the success of each member.

In *Developing the Leader Within You*, John Maxwell explains what inspires people to make *your* vision *their* vision:

- **"Significant contributions**
  People must see value in what they are doing. They want to pursue a cause that will have a lasting impact.
- **Goal participation**
  People support what they create. This builds team spirit, enhances morale, and helps everyone feel important.
- **Positive dissatisfaction**
  In one word, that is motivation. Frustration is always a sign that you have vision.
- **Recognition**
  People want to be noticed.
- **Clear expectations**
  People are motivated when they know exactly what they are to do."

Make the commitment today that you aren't going to work alone. Harness the power that comes from building a team and you'll enjoy the benefits.

Locate Your Top Team

> The first method for estimating the intelligence of a ruler is to look at the men he has around him.
> —Niccolo Machiavelli

How important are the right people to your vision? Statistics report that 20 percent of people in an organization will be responsible for 80 percent of the company's success.

Are you connected with the right people who will assist you, be honest with you, believe in you, support you, stretch you, and accelerate you toward your dreams? Your top 20 percent are the influencers on your team. They are the producers closest to you. They are the decision-makers, the problem-solvers, and the highly proactive team players around you.

"The smaller the organization, the more

important the hiring." This phrase has resonated with me since the day I read it in John Maxwell's book, *Developing the Leader Within You*. It is vital that you choose the most qualified, proactive influencers for your team.

In order to identify your top 20 percent you need to make a list of every person directly connected to you (in your company, on your team, in your immediate sphere of influence).

Then ask yourself this question about each one: "If this person withdrew their support, what kind of impact would it have on my life?"

If you wouldn't be able to function without their support, put a check next to their name. If their absence would nearly devastate your progress, put a check next to their name. If business would continue running as usual without them, do not put a check next to their name.

You will most likely come up with about 20 percent of the people as your highest influencers, highest leaders, and highest producers. And remember, people are your most valuable asset. God is going to bring you people who have strengths in the areas of your greatest weaknesses. That's exactly what you need.

I highly recommend applying the "DiSC Profile Test" to your team. DiSC helps a team understand their behavioral differences and where each member places importance on results. This is an excellent assessment tool used by more than 40 million people to improve teamwork and communication. It's helpful to know the individual characteristics of each team member. This test can be acquired online and should be taken by each member of your top team.

- **D = Dominance**: this person places emphasis on results, the bottom line, and confidence.
    Behaviors of Dominance:
    - Sees the big picture
    - Can be blunt
    - Accepts challenges
    - Gets straight to the point
- **I = Influence:** this person places emphasis on influencing or persuading others, openness, and relationships.
    Behaviors of Influence:
    - Shows enthusiasm
    - Is optimistic
    - Likes to collaborate

- Dislikes being ignored
- **S= Steadiness:** this person places emphasis on cooperation, sincerity, and dependability.
  Behaviors of Steadiness:
  - Doesn't like to be rushed
  - Calm manner
  - Calm approach
  - Supportive actions
  - Humility
- **C= Conscientiousness**: this person places emphasis on quality and accuracy, expertise, and competency.
  Behaviors of Conscientiousness:
  - Enjoys independence
  - Objective reasoning
  - Wants the details
  - Fears being wrong[5]

Surround yourself with people who think differently than you. It's great to create an environment where different opinions are valued. This is how great ideas are born.

There are many other valuable tests you can

---

5 DiSC overview, (https://discprofile.com/what-is-disc/overview/).

access as you develop your top team. Invest the time to do this. Those around you will appreciate your interest in them, and you will be better equipped to communicate with each member by knowing their individual styles, behaviors, and preferences.

Develop Your Team

> Those closest to the leader will determine
> the level of success for that leader.
> —John Maxwell

If you want to grow your business, grow your people. Most leaders look to increase production in order for the company to grow. However, if you want to experience significant growth, invest in your team.

This concept is the difference between asking, "What can I get out of my team?" and "How can I invest in them?" This latter thinking places a high premium on training your closest team members. A leader is best judged by his or her followers. That's right (and may be scary for some of you). A leader can be evaluated by the people he or she leads. This can be a challenge and may demand a shift in your thinking if you believe that you, as a leader, need to know and do it all.

In order to achieve greater success in your business, you must place a high priority on developing the people that God brings to you. Once you have built your team of the top 20 percent of influencers, producers, and leaders that are already around you, you are responsible for pouring yourself into them.

In *Developing the Leader Within You*, John Maxwell advises that leaders:

- determine which people are the top 20% producers;
- spend 80% of their "people time" with the top 20%; and
- spend 80% of personal developmental dollars on the top 20%.

John Maxwell advises leaders to expose team members to great books, great places, great people, and great events. (In Chapter 5, "Establish a Learning Culture," I will share more about how I began developing leaders on my team with a plan for "accelerated growth.")

Schedule field trips to various businesses, conferences, or outfits already doing what you desire to do. I have taken my teams to live tapings of *Life Today* with James and Betty Robison to help our media department enlarge their vision. I have taken production teams to Joyce Meyer conferences to view their exhibits. Our organization has chartered buses for the whole staff to attend "Get Motivated" conferences to hear speakers such as George W. Bush, Colin Powell, Rudy Guiliani, and Zig Ziglar. Investing in your team is an investment in the growth of your business.

Build a mindset that everything you do as a leader is purposed to teach, train, coach, and mentor your team. Your team is there to provide wise counsel for you. Ask for their input, opinions, and recommendations before you make major decisions. They bring diversity to your business, and that's a good thing.

Dr. Dean Radtke defines the job description of top leaders (or CEOs) as such:

1. Provide direction.
2. Obtain plans, ideas, and recommendations (from your team).
3. Commission the work (empower them).
4. Provide success (coach, teach, train and mentor your team).
5. Obtain evaluation.

> The more people you develop, the greater the extent of your dreams.
> —John Maxwell

Once I determined the top influencers in my organization, I assigned them to a major department in the company. Always place your top leaders in charge of your organization's highest priorities.

My next step was to appoint a regular meeting time with them each week. I established the expectation that we adhere to our set meetings, no matter what. I knew I had to make an investment of my time and resources to train them.

To be perfectly honest, I was very naïve in the area of leadership and developing teams. I did not have this concept modeled for me; therefore, I felt very vulnerable. Rather than act and appear inadequate, I took on the challenge to grow *myself* as I began growing my team.

The last thing I want you to do is get overwhelmed. In Chapter 5 I will show you, in very elementary stages, how I began developing my team one book, one page, and one day at a time.

Empower your team

> The best executive is the one who has sense enough to pick good men to do what he wants done, and self-restraint to keep from meddling with them while they do it.
> —Theodore Roosevelt

When a directive is given to a well-trained team, each member takes ownership in the assignment and team members feel comfortable solving problems and brainstorming solutions.

Empower your team to become problem-solvers. Teach them to never bring problems to you without a solution; otherwise, they are just complaining. Remember, as the leader your job is to provide direction while your team provides solutions.

A big percentage of your time in meetings will be spent asking questions. Yes, you, the leader of the team, need to spend more time asking questions and empowering your team to problem solve.

If someone comes to you with a problem, your reply should be, "What do you recommend we do?" Put the ball back in their court. Your job isn't to figure out every solution; your job is to hear the recommendations and give direction.

I have never gone to my dad as his CEO and said, "The purchasing department made an error on the new book purchase and ordered 10,000 too many! We just wasted tons of money. What do you think we should do?"

I have never scheduled a meeting with him to discuss a challenge without offering several recommendations (brought to me by my top leaders). This type of thinking requires training. As the leader, you have to communicate this new mindset among your team, and it will need to be repeated continually until they no longer bring problems alone. They present the challenge and they are ready to offer their well-thought-out recommendations to fix it. This is empowering.

If your goal is to see your seminars grow by 20 percent over the next twelve months, then begin by establishing exactly what 20 percent means, thus clearly communicating the vision. For example: *Our last conference held 1,000 attendees. We want to see 1,200 in attendance this year (twenty percent growth).*

Then begin asking questions.
- *When you first attended one of our conferences, what inspired you to come back?*
    - List the responses and identify the causes.
- *What are some solutions we can provide to overcome that?*
    - List ideas.

You set the directions; your team provides solutions. It causes those around you to take ownership in the success of the next conference because it was *their* ideas that you approved in order to see growth. In fact, they will work tirelessly to prove to you that they had a great idea! Your team needs to know that you believe in them.

When I was seven years old, I remember overhearing my aunt and mother sitting in the

Don't be vague w/ Goals ~ give exact details.

kitchen talking about me. They didn't know I was nearby and could hear their conversation.

"Terri Lynn is so smart, isn't she?" said Aunt Jan. My mom replied, "She really is a smart little girl."

Subconsciously or consciously, I remember thinking *I need to be smart to live up to what they think about me.*

As a result, I made the Dean's List nearly every semester of college and graduated with honors and a Bachelor of Arts degree from Texas Tech University. I know that their words were deposited in me to produce the results I strove for all of my educational life.

Your team needs to know that you believe in them. They need to hear it. They have gifts and talents that you don't have. A secure leader points them out and acknowledges them for it. An insecure leader has to have all the praise; they must feel like the smartest, the most educated, and the person with the greatest ideas in the room. When you lead in that manner, you simply attract robots that do what you say but do not take ownership of your vision.

Build belief in your team.

Acknowledge & praise gifts others have.

62

Your job is to never take your eyes off the vision, find people who are qualified in areas of expertise that you need, and then empower them to make it happen. The number one thing people want in the workplace is an opportunity to make a difference. Tap into the wisdom of those around you and allow them to join in the vision.

Appreciate Your Team

> It's wonderful when the people believe in their leader; it's more wonderful when the leader believes in the people.
> —John C. Maxwell

In a recent study on reasons employees leave a company, 46% said they do so because they feel unappreciated; 61% said their bosses don't place very much importance on them as people, and 88% said they do not receive acknowledgement for the work they do. Appreciation is important. Acknowledging appreciation is *very* important.

In fact, in another management survey asking 200 companies what motivates their employees, out of a list of ten possible things, appreciation is the number-one motivator!

I have been told that there are three kinds of appreciation: auditory, visual, and kinesthetic. There is a type of appreciation that means the most to each person.

- Auditory people need to be told verbally how much they are appreciated. If you give a hand-written thank you note to an auditory person, they may feel discouraged that you didn't even take the time to call them or stop them in the hallway to say thanks.
- Visual people need to receive something they can see, set on their desk, hang on their wall, or keep in their home. They enjoy receiving flowers, cards, awards, pictures, trophies, and gifts that serve as reminders of appreciation.
- Kinesthetic people prefer to feel the gratitude. A simple handshake, a hug, a pat on the back, or doing something with them means the world to them. It could involve taking them to lunch or dinner, grabbing coffee together, going to a game or a concert. They need to feel and experience the appreciation.

people receive appreciation in different ways

When it comes to your team, you have to learn which style of appreciation means most to each person and go out of your way to speak the language of appreciation they prefer.

Warning: Being a member on a Top Team carries with it increased responsibility.

Your team players need to know up front that along with accepting the "parking spot with their name on it," they agree to elevate the level of their work performance as well. The higher your climb in a company or organization, more is expected and required from you in terms of learning, growing, achieving results, developing others, creating change, earning respect, and more. You help set the example for others to follow so everything you do matters even more.

Finding and building your team reflects your leadership. Make the investment, take the time, and do it right.

Chapter Four

4
Consistently Meet with Your Team

> There is a secret power that drives some businesses to succeed, and this secret power can be summed up in one word: consistency.
>
> —Kim Morris

Consistency is the difference between failure and success. I have determined to be consistent about consistency because it:

- creates effective communication,
- solves problems,
- creates clear vision,
- demonstrates respect for your team, and
- creates a positive reputation.

1. **Consistently meeting with your team creates effective communication.**

> When the eagles are silent, the parrots
> begin to jabber.
> —Winston Churchill

In the book of Genesis, there's a story of ungodly men attempting to build a tower (The Tower of Babel) to reach heaven. They were succeeding in this seemingly impossible dream until God mixed up their languages. Yes, that's where French, Spanish, Portuguese, German, even Cajun-speaking people began to babble. As a result, the project was never completed.

From this story, we learn the importance of communication. When we cannot communicate clearly, progress disappears. In this story, the vision, the dream, and the goal came to a complete stop simply because the people could not effectively speak to one another. The same is true in a company. When your team meets haphazardly, unplanned, or irregularly, the communication will most definitely be affected in a negative way.

At the onset of becoming CEO, I met one-on-one with each member of my staff to hear their hearts and frustrations, as well as their desires and dreams for the organization. I asked them to share with me what their greatest frustrations were in working at our company. It was oddly unanimous how often I heard the same two resounding complaints: (1) a lack of communication and (2) a lack of planning.

I interpreted those complaints to mean there was an overall lack of vision. Direction. This is where I knew to focus my attention. First, I established consistent communication with our entire staff through monthly meetings. Once I built my team of top leaders (directors) who work directly with me, I scheduled weekly meetings with them. Without fail, each Wednesday from 9:30 a.m.-12:00 p.m., we meet to ensure every person is crystal clear on everything that is happening.

In our monthly staff meetings (which I refer to as "Pep Rallies"), I communicate with our team and have my directors share reports, progress, and testimonials. The purpose is to be clear as a team on what we are doing and where we are going. Ultimately, we want to prevent "babbling."

One of the most disrespectful actions you can take toward your staff is to neglect to communicate direction, updates, and progress with them. If the

[handwritten margin note: Both need to exist for a business to thrive, and they need to be communicated]

outside world knows more information about your organization before some of your staff does, it demonstrates a lack of respect.

I would never want my team to discover my latest book launch while scrolling through social media posts. Those working closest to you need to know what is going on before any news is communicated publicly.

Consistency creates effective communication. Do what you need to do in order to schedule and adhere to a consistent meeting with your team. Trust me, there are times when I am in no mood to facilitate my weekly team meetings. I have been scheduled to fly overseas on occasion, but I still attended the scheduled weekly meeting because consistency is critical.

2. Consistently meeting with your team solves problems.

> I not only use all the brains I have, but all I can borrow.
> —Woodrow Wilson

I'll never forget the day I met with my top leaders to communicate a new, urgent vision. It wasn't the vision I was known for casting.

"I have some new direction that we must focus on and, as a team, I want you to help me reach this goal," I said.

With excitement in their eyes to chase after a new target, I pulled out a sheet of paper with $120,000 typed in a giant, bold, red font!

Was it a financial goal for a new TV time slot? Was it a purchase order for new books? Was it a vision for new software for customer service? Was it the cost to underwrite the annual budget for an orphanage in Africa?

I continued, "We must reduce our expenses by $120,000. Per. Month!"

Not for the year, not for the first quarter. Per month.

I admitted, "I don't have a clue how to achieve this goal, but I believe God has gifted you to help solve problems in this organization, and we are going to come together as a team to reach this vision."

No doubt this was a huge challenge, but one that my team knew I believed they could conquer;

therefore, a certain level of enthusiasm and determination arose. They were actually excited to—yes, that's right—reduce spending!

I believe in my team's ability to discover solutions that I would never consider, to brainstorm ideas that I would never toss around, and to hear from God as much as I do. Because I believe in them to this degree, they always rise to the occasion. People tend to become what the most important people in their lives think they will become.

My directors took on this intense financial challenge. As a team, we met consistently to discover a gambit of solutions that enabled us to decrease monthly expenditures, solutions that I would have never recognized without their input.

In many organizations, the CEO makes all the decisions without receiving input from his colleagues. Unfortunately, in a stressful financial situation they look for the highest expense in the company, which, in many cases, is the salary or compensation of employees. When money is tight, they feel that there is no other solution to examine; they must terminate positions. That is always the last solution I want to consider.

My team offered solutions for reducing expenses such as:

- Produce our magazine digitally only for two issues. This reduced the cost of printing issues *and* shipping magazines for two full issues.
- Eliminate one TV network from our broadcast time slot, which had the smallest coverage and wasn't producing the greatest return on investment.
- Switch our website hosting company with one that utilizes other online streaming sources.
- Change the way we were printing our shipping labels (which saved us $2,000 per month).

Through consistency, my team achieved this ambitious goal over a period of several months. Not only did we decrease our monthly expenses, we also increased our monthly income.

Many insecure leaders sit at their desks alone and rack their brains trying to examine and solve all the company's problems without input from anyone else. Had I done that, I would still be sitting at my beautiful black desk, to this day, trying to figure out this financial puzzle.

Allow the team to help to find a solution.

You were never meant to lead alone. Allow your team members to get involved in the brainstorming, problem solving, and creative thinking process. Utilize their gifts. Gain wisdom from them. Listen to their ideas. Evaluate their solutions. Consistently meet with them. Doing all these things enables you to be free to lead and effectively do what you are called to do.

As your business or organization grows, you simply cannot be involved in every aspect at the same level you may have been in the past. But you must stay informed of what is happening in order to provide direction.

If your toilet has a leak and water is flooding the bathroom, whom do you call? The president of the plumbing company? No. You call the plumber who works for the company. He inspects the problem. He provides solutions. The president hasn't actually fixed a toilet in twenty years! He just runs the company.

Your team sees things you do not see anymore. From your position of leading, you are no longer on the ground floor dealing with the day-to-day issues. Your team has ideas and solutions that you can't see. Listen to them.

3. Consistently meeting with your team creates clear vision.

Is the vision clear to your team? Or are you the only one who sees it? You may have your vision clear and on paper but does your staff, congregation, partners, or team members know that vision? There is a big difference!

If you're the only one who knows the vision, you're not going to go very far! It's important to know your vision *and* communicate it consistently.

In the first few months as CEO of Jerry Savelle Ministries, I really wanted to be clear on the vision for each area of our organization: the international department, the publications department, the television department, the missions outreach, the book publishing division, everything.

Starting with the missions department of the organization, I pulled a group of creative people together from our media, marketing, and public relations departments. I handed each of them a piece of paper and a pen and gave a directive: "I want each of you to write down what *you believe* this organization is doing around the world in missions. Just tell me what you think our vision is for the missions' outreach of this ministry." They began to write.

After a few minutes, I asked them to turn their papers in anonymously. One by one, I began to read the responses aloud. I received the following statements:

- We are called to provide school desks for deaf children in Tanzania.
- We give free haircuts and provide food for the elderly in Malaysia.
- We donate soccer balls and uniforms to help the less fortunate kids in Singapore.
- We help train pastors in Kenya.
- We rescue children from the dumpster areas of Thailand.

Every single response was different! What did that communicate to me? The vision was not clear! At all! And if my own staff does not have a clue what our vision is for this department, then what does the rest of the world think? What do the partners and contributors of our organization think if we don't even know what we're doing?

I used that assignment to bring clarity to this one department. I simply began to pray and ask the Lord for the vision of our missions department and what he was instructing us to do. Vision always starts in prayer and thought. It's where you find clues.

In my time spent praying over our vision for missions, I began to think of my mother. When she was a little girl already seeking God to direct her life, she heard the Lord tell her she would marry a man who would preach the Gospel and go to Africa when she grew up.

Mom always said, "We're going to Africa. We're going to reach Africa." So, my search for answers was becoming clearer. I wrote that important clue down.

Then I remembered when my dad began preaching back in 1969. The first mission trip he ever launched was to Africa. When he first stepped foot on African soil, God deposited a desire and a dream in his heart to reach the people for Jesus. I wrote that clue down.

Over time, our organization began doing so many mission works that we lost sight of that original vision to focus on Africa. We were doing a broad variety of small things literally all over the world rather than making one big impact in one area.

I continued to pray, and then I met with my dad to obtain direction. I said, "Dad, what do you think about us aiming all of our efforts to do everything we can to reach the continent of Africa?" My dad looked at me and said, "Let's get Africa back. That's where this ministry started, and that's where we're going to finish." Well, that's all I needed to hear.

I met with the staff immediately and confidently communicated that the mission field of Jerry Savelle Ministries is Africa.

"Let's be crystal clear on our mission; it's Africa. And we are going to do everything God tells us to do in order to impact Africa," I said.

Once the direction was clearly mapped out for our team, they began brainstorming ideas, offering solutions, and running with purpose. We began developing our own Bible study curriculum (translated into Kiswahili) to train pastors all over Africa. We launched our curriculum and began training 300 African pastors in Tanzania in the first year! When the vision is clear, the provision will appear. Read that statement again. It is true in every area of life.

In 2008, I attended the first graduation ceremony in Arusha, Tanzania. Sitting under a dome in hot, smoldering temperatures, watching 300 African pastors in emerald green caps and gowns smiling proudly as they walked down the aisle to celebrate their most outstanding accomplishment, I glanced over at my dad on the front row in his Chancellor's robe and noticed he was hunched over crying at the reality of his dream to impact these precious people and make a mark on their nation.

I stood there praising God under my breath for giving me the direction to clarify this vision and then communicate it to a team who could walk it out and produce these kinds of results.

When the vision or direction of your team isn't identified and communicated properly, then every idea sounds good and you and your team will become easily distracted. You have a tendency to drift from one activity to another. You come to the end of the year and simply wonder, *What did we do?*

> Find a man or woman who lacks motivation and I'll show you someone with little or no vision.
> —Andy Stanley

When your team knows the vision, it creates enthusiasm. When they get enthusiastic about a purpose, they develop ambition! Ambition leads to results.

4. Consistency demonstrates respect for your team.

> Tell me, and I'll forget. Show me, and I may not remember. Involve me and I'll understand.
> —Native American Proverb

It's been said that the number one thing people want in the workplace is the opportunity to make a difference. God didn't anoint you to know it all.

I read a statistic years ago from the CEO workshop with Dr. Dean Radtke that said 40% of small businesses fail the first year and 80% fail by the fifth year. Why is this? Because entrepreneurs are doing all the work and are never empowered by their teams. They should have been leading, not doing.

As a leader, your role is to give direction. Your team's role is to provide the solutions, ideas, and recommendations to carry out your direction. Remember, the people you have surrounded yourself with are problem solvers. If you are taking on all of their work, solving every problem, providing every idea, then you are actually depriving them of using the gifts God has given them.

By consistently meeting with your team, you will recognize more of their unique gifts, strengths, and contributions to your organization. If your meetings are random and infrequent, you may not ever grasp the very solutions God has brought to support you.

> *Leadership* determines the direction of the company. *Organization* determines the potential of the company. *Personnel* determine the success of the company.
> —John C. Maxwell

Don't be selfish! Allow others to help.

I heard the late Lester Sumrall share an insightful message on the story of the strongest man in the Bible, Samson. Unfortunately, the strongest man who ever lived has forever gone down in history for his weakness.

In this talk, Sumrall revealed that Samson's weakness (Delilah) gained power over him because he was alone. He wasn't accountable to anyone. He chose to be alone, to do everything alone, to lead alone. He would not listen to anyone. He thought he was strong enough to do it alone, and so he did. However, when temptation came, he had no wise counsel warning him, urging him to avoid it and to stay focused.

We need each other. Develop relationships with your team by communicating often with the people who believe in your vision. This demostrates great respect for your team.

- Invest in them.
- Recognize them.
- Appreciate them.
- Listen to them.
- Coach them.
- Believe in them.

5. Consistently meeting with your team creates a positive reputation.

> It may seem simple, but consistently taking the right action is the key to creating success in nearly any worthwhile venture.
> —Melanie Dunn Ethridge

To be described as "consistent" is a great compliment. Whether it is referring to your exercise regime, your foreign language studies, your ability to save money, your maintenance of a clean home, your daily Bible reading, or your arrival to meetings on time, consistency is the key to a positive reputation.

As a leader, you want to be respected by your team. One of the best ways to make this happen is through consistency. If you determine that you will meet with your team twice each month, then rain or shine, you meet with them twice each month (even if it's for 10 minutes!). You do whatever you need to do in order to keep that commitment with them.

83

Over a period of time, you will develop a reputation worth emulating. Remember, what you do consistently will communicate a message to your colleagues, friends, and family of what they can expect from you. You want their expectations to be positive.

> It's not what we do once in a while
> that shapes our lives. It's what we do
> consistently.
> — Anthony Robbins

A lack of consistency creates insecurity. When you announce what you plan to do, but do not follow up with your actions, you not only break trust with yourself but with your colleagues. After a series of broken commitments, you subconsciously begin to doubt your own promises and commitments, which then affects your personal self-esteem and security. And nobody wants to follow an insecure leader.

Every day you will be confronted with a myriad of distractions and urgent responsibilities that are designed to steal you from your priorities. You must decide ahead of time where you want to be consistent and schedule it on your calendar. As a result, when you commit to doing something over and over (whether you feel like it or not), your personal confidence grows as well as the team's confidence in you.

Chapter Five

5

Establish a Learning Culture

> Growing employees make growing companies.
> —John Maxwell

Years ago, I was sitting quietly, thinking and praying about the future of our organization when I heard these words in my heart: "Accelerated growth is a must among your leaders."

Accelerated (Merriam Webster dictionary): to hasten the progress, to cause to move faster, to speed up and to enable to complete a course in less than usual time.

Up until that moment, I had no plan for developing leaders on my team. I had built a strong team, cast vision to them, met with them consistently, but I had no intentional, strategic plan for *their* growth.

After God spoke those words to my heart, I wasted no time planning my team members' acceleration. I went to the local bookstore and purchased seven copies of John Maxwell's book, *Developing the Leader Within You,* as well as seven blank journals and pens.

Book → to read

My fifteen-year-old nephew, Preston, was staying with our family that weekend when I received the direction for my team's growth. I watched him read an entire 200-page book in a single weekend, in the midst of swimming, eating out, watching television, and hanging out with us. That inspired me!

I went to work the next week with my books, journals, pens, and a plan. I met with my team and shared that we would begin a learning journey together, that it would not only cause us to grow as individuals, but that our company would also grow as a result.

I passed the leadership materials out to each director and said, "I want you to read this entire book by next Wednesday (seven days from then) and journal the highlights from each chapter in your own personal executive journal."

The plan was to meet with them in one week to discuss this new knowledge.

"One week?" Someone asked.

"You want us to read this whole book in one week?" Another team member piped up.

"Yes," I answered. "Accelerated growth is a must."

The protests rang loud and clear. "But this is a big book!"

I then explained how my nephew was able to read an entire book in a weekend. Why? He desired to. He wanted to. How do you change desires? By changing what you give attention to. As we give more attention to educating ourselves as leaders, our desires begin to change. Little by little, we will desire learning, reading, growing ourselves. And that is exactly what happened!

One week later, we joined for our weekly meeting with journals full of wisdom. The team looked different. They looked full. They looked inspired. They looked eager to share what they discovered.

We started with Chapter 1. Without pointing to any one person and making them feel uncomfortable, I simply asked the group what they learned. One-by-one they began to share. The room overflowing with conversation, I finally had to interrupt the discussion to move on to Chapter 2. It was intriguing to watch them refer to handwritten notes in their journals of all this newfound wisdom and knowledge they (and I) were discovering.

Two hours later, as we had completed each chapter with a thorough discussion, you could see the question on everyone's face: *What's our next assignment?*

You will be amazed at how strongly your team desires direction from you. They want to be challenged. They want opportunities to grow. They want vision.

I was thrilled to have already prepared my team's next assignment—another leadership book, *The Seven Habits of Highly Effective People*, by Stephen Covey. However, this time I required the reading of only two chapters by the following Wednesday.

Book to read

Each week, year after year, I created a plan for their growth. Often times, the direction was to listen to one audio message and journal the points that stood out to them. The topics ranged from money management, vision, growth, fasting, staff development, and faith. Each of my leaders will testify to this—we are not the same people we used to be.

Provide a Growth Environment

There is a certain species of fish that adapts to its environment. If you place this fish in a tiny aquarium, it will stay small. But if you release it into a large body of water, it will grow to its intended size. People are the same way. If your team is exposed to a small, limited-thinking environment, they will stay small. However, if you challenge them to grow and enlarge their thinking as well as expose them to opportunities for growth, then they and your organization will grow to its intended size. They dream bigger. They plan bigger. They do bigger.

Your entire team needs to be always growing. And you, as the leader, must provide the environment for growth. I've never met anyone on my team who despised growing. They love educating themselves. And I'm so proud of them when I hear them talk with wisdom they've gained from their plans for personal growth. And it is happening on every level in our organization.

Our maintenance department reads books on leadership, on excellence, and on finances. Our entire staff is reading Dave Ramsey's *Total Money Makeover*. Our customer service department reads books on sales, marketing, and relationship building. Our production department also reads books on sales and marketing.

Whether you run a business, lead a ministry or department, or pastor a church or youth group, establish a learning culture. Give those you lead a challenge to read, to grow, to stretch. Meet with them consistently and hold them accountable. Whatever you do, never give an assignment without a follow-up plan. Hold them, and yourself, accountable. Schedule meetings with them to discuss what they have learned. And don't rush through the follow up. Take your time.

Growth is what happens when you expose your team to growing opportunities. They will light up with new ideas. They will surprise you with knowledge. They will outthink you. They will surpass previous progress in record time!

There was a canvas company that supplied material for tents, duffle bags, sails and other items for which sturdiness is required. Years ago someone in the purchasing department made a huge error by placing too many zeroes on the purchase agreement. When the order arrived, a load of canvas was unloaded and overflowed the entire warehouse. Not knowing how to proceed with this enormous error, someone in the warehouse had an idea: *What if we made pants out of the canvas?*

His colleagues laughed saying, "You can't make pants out of canvas. Nobody would wear that." Well, that was the beginning of blue jeans— somebody in the warehouse had an idea.

The people you have surrounded yourself with are going to get ideas that you would never get, so you need to continually encourage them to think, to dream, and to enlarge their capacity to grow.

Establish a learning culture in your company, your church, your ministry, or your organization. Give them challenges. Send them on field trips. Take them to seminars. Enroll them in classes. Expose them to other great leaders.

Also, you don't have to spend a ton of money doing these things. You can expose your team to growth opportunities in many cost-effective ways. For example, once a month, my entire staff meets as a group to learn. Many times, we watch leadership podcasts from YouTube. The videos are free to watch; the investment, priceless!

Everyone Needs a Coach

> You will never maximize your potential in any area without coaching. It is impossible.
> — Andy Stanley
> *The Next Generation Leader*

Today you often hear the term "success coach." In fact, I am considered one to some young ladies I mentor. I love that word, "coach." In Kevin Hall's book, *Aspire*, he explains how the word "coach" originated from the horse-drawn coaches that were developed in the town of Kocs during the fifteenth century. These vehicles not only transported royalty but valuables, mail, and common passengers as well.

Kevin Hall wrote, "A 'coach' remains something, or someone, who carries a valued person from where they are to where they want to be." In other words, if you had a coach, you knew you would end up at your destination.

You and your team need your very own coach. You need someone helping you to grow, improve, increase, enlarge, and reach your destination.

Coaches may actually be people you will never meet in person. One of the best ways to "hire" one is to simply read their books and listen to their audio messages. In his book, *15 Invaluable Laws of Growth*, John Maxwell talks about the coaches who have influenced his life through their writing.

> Dale Carnegie taught me people skills when I read *How to Win Friends and Influence People* in junior high school. James Allen helped me understand that my attitude and the way that I thought would impact the course of my life when I read *As a Man Thinketh*. And Oswald Sanders revealed the importance of leadership to me for the first time when I read his book *Spiritual Leadership*.

It is important that you find someone you connect with—that you can receive from. You may have approximately three to five people who *really* speak to you more than others. Those are divine connections. There may be a certain minister or motivational speaker whom you identify with so much that you feel you know them personally. God will purposefully bring mentors across your path that inspire you to do more, to be more, to have more.

Honor your preferences when it comes to different teaching styles. You gravitate to certain people for a reason. Start receiving from them consistently! There are mentors who specialize in certain areas of improvement such as health and fitness, financial security, dreams and goals, faith in God, emotional healing, leadership and success. Determine in which areas you need to spend more time learning and from whom. Make a decision to connect with people who have more experience than you and can help in your endeavors.

To know the road ahead, ask those
coming back.
—Chinese Proverb

We can benefit from the experience of others. In fact, most successful people love telling their stories and offering their wisdom. You simply have to ask.

> Anyone who walks with wise people grows wise. But a companion of foolish people suffers harm.
> —Proverbs 13:20 NIV

In my first year as a CEO, I knew I needed wisdom and needed it fast. Right off the bat, I made a phone call to a very large ministry and asked for a thirty-minute appointment with the CEO of that organization. He agreed to meet. I walked into his office prepared with my list of questions. I think he enjoyed sharing his wisdom with me even more than I enjoyed hearing it. This man offered life-changing information that guided me in the right direction.

Next, I called Jesse Duplantis' office in New Orleans, Louisiana. I had already signed up to attend his upcoming conference, but asked if I could also pick his brain for about thirty minutes. Our families are close friends, but I wanted to learn from him as a businessman and minister. I prepared for the meeting with a typed list of questions. I learned such valuable information from Jesse that I still reflect on to this day.

Another time, I contacted the former CEO of The Gap. I wanted to hear his business advice for structuring an organization. He graciously agreed to meet me and listen to my questions. I cannot even describe how much his wisdom has equipped me to do what I am doing today.

Get Out of Your Comfort Zone

It can be intimidating to approach people who have more experience or greater positions or success, but it's necessary for your own growth! Your comfort zone is similar to a prison. It keeps you confined and limited. If you want to go to the next level in your business or ministry, you will feel uncomfortable from time to time. I want you to view that awkward feeling in your pit as a good thing. It means change!

Fear is normal. Whenever you do something new, you will experience the uneasy feeling of the unknown. Some people will go to great lengths to avoid that feeling. They will give up on their dreams, let people walk all over them, settle for a lower salary, and remain stuck in a rut. Don't let that be you!

On purpose, put yourself in as many uncomfortable situations as possible. Take whatever steps are necessary to stretch yourself in the area of your associations and connections. Ask for appointments. Offer to take those individuals to lunch or dinner. Sign up for their workshop or conference. If you are only given ten or fifteen minutes of their time, be prepared with a list of questions. The only way to grow is to step out of your comfort zone.

> Mentors don't like to have their time wasted. When you seek out their advice... follow it.
>
> —Jack Canfield

We ask family members, co-workers, neighbors, and friends for advice in areas they may not have experience in. Mentors are essential in our lives for this reason. Seek out opportunities to learn from someone with a wealth of knowledge and resources. Research businesses that are succeeding in your area of interest, search online, attend workshops and seminars, and go prepared to learn.

Never show up expecting someone to just teach you everything they know. Ask good questions and listen to what they have to say. Listen. Listen. Listen. You are there to learn, not talk about yourself. Be interested; don't try to be interesting.

Make the Most of Your Minutes

> Most people who decide to grow personally find their first mentors in the pages of books.
> —John Maxwell

Since we become like those we spend the most time with, we should choose our mentors wisely.

By simply listening to their CDs, you will begin to talk like them. In reading their books, you will begin to think like them. In watching and observing their mannerisms, you will begin to imitate them.

Pastor Erik Lawson is a friend of mine who pastors one of the fastest growing churches in America. He recently said at the Heritage of Faith Ministers' Conference, "I have *spent time* with Bill Gates, Donald Trump, John Maxwell, T.D. Jakes, and Stephen Covey." We looked at him with our mouths wide open. Then he said, "But I've never met any of them."

Pastor Erik continued, "However, I *spend time* with them on my way to work and on my way home, day in and day out."

According to "The Atlantic," the American commuter spends 38 hours a year stuck in traffic! Like Pastor Erik, successful people find learning opportunities everywhere—like during their commute to and from work. Teach your team (and you do the same) to turn their car into a classroom. Your team will never view their morning commute as wasted time again. They will grow tremendously as a result of this simple discipline and may actually enjoy getting stuck in traffic as a result!

My dear friend, Pastor Brendan White, leads a thriving church in the heart of Paris, France. During one of my ministry trips to his church, he was stuck in Paris traffic for six hours! Out of compassion, I said, "Brendan, you seem so content. Were you frustrated?"

He replied, "First of all, I'm in Paris. How can I complain?" (I totally agree with that!) Then he said, "It gave me six hours to build my faith! I'm exploding inside!"

Teach your team to view their time spent in a car as a time to grow. Borrow audio messages from friends, download messages onto their phones, purchase fresh, new teaching and have them place them in their cars. Set them up to succeed.

Chapter Six

6

Know Your Core Values

When you know your core values, every
decision you make is easier. Sound core
values are the foundation of a truly
successful business.
—Stephen Covey

An organization's core values and the culture
those values create will determine whether or not
its vision and goals are accomplished. It is possible
to have a strong, clear vision, communicate
it effectively, but have a culture in place that
is counter-productive to effectiveness. If your
desire is to be a cutting-edge, risk-taking, creative
organization, it won't happen if your values
and culture reinforce playing it safe and merely
maintaining what you've already achieved.

For many years, our organization had
internal, unspoken core values, and the team
was expected to uphold those values. However,

without verbally and definitively communicating the values of the organization, our team relied on personal assumptions rather than a collective belief. Values must be defined and understood in order for a team to function properly.

Defining Core Values

Core values are the driving force behind the way you do what you do in your organization. They are the guiding principles that dictate the behaviors and actions of yourself and your colleagues as well as the procedures for your business, company, or team.

Your core values are the practices you adhere to in order to fulfill your vision. They clarify who you are and what your organization stands for. In an ever-changing world, it is necessary that your core values remain constant.

As I began educating myself in leadership, I became acutely aware that defining and communicating core values is vital to a company's success. So, I began to narrow down the essential practices for which our company stood.

When my father worked for Kenneth Copeland in the early 1970s, Mr. Copeland taught him three core values:

1. Be excellent.
2. Be on time.
3. Have integrity.

I adopted those three values as part of our core values and added one more, creating the acronym T.I.E.S.

> Timeliness
> Integrity
> Excellence
> Smiles

In order to vividly and visually communicate this essential practice in our company, I asked our Director of Human Resources to purchase the ugliest ties she could find, one for each staff member in our organization. At our next monthly staff meeting, I brought everyone together to teach and instill the core values of our company in a memorable, practical way.

Timeliness requires us to be on time in every area. Show up to work on time. Answer the phone on time. Respond to emails on time. Ship the products on time. Arrive at the event on time. Start the event on time. We plan ahead, we are prepared, and we are ready for opportunities that come our way. Timeliness is something that we stand for in every department and function of this organization.

Integrity means that there is consistency between what we say and what we do. We practice what we preach. We are the same people in public as we are when nobody is looking. We follow through with what we say we will do. If we say that an order will be shipped within 48 hours, we keep our word even to our own hurt. Integrity is character that stems from a condition of the heart.

Excellence means that we are committed to continuous improvement. We never settle for average or good enough. Average is as close to the bottom as it is to the top. Excellence means that we are consistently educating ourselves, growing, and stretching to the next level. We are excellent in our physical appearance, our workspace, our products, our publications, our facilities, and our environment.

Smiles represent an outward display of an inward decision to be positive. No matter how things may look, we choose to be positive because we firmly believe that God is in control. We stay optimistic because our faith is in our faithful God who is on our side. We have smiles on our faces because we trust God in every area of our lives. We have a good, positive attitude when dealing with vendors, donors, customers, and other employees because we want our organization to be a testament to the joy of God's faithfulness.

After explaining these core values, I "crowned" each employee with an ugly tie. (Humor always adds more fun to a staff meeting.) They are required to wear their "ugly tie" to each and every staff meeting now. They can wear them any way they want. It brings a little craziness to the monthly meeting when your team walks in with a tie around their head, their waist, their arm, or imitating a woman's scarf.

The reason we continue this tradition is so every single employee will remember—and never forget—the core values of our organization. Making something memorable makes it last. Communicate the core values for your organization in a way that causes your team to adopt them and stand for them.

We celebrate and reinforce our values consistently. Besides wearing our ties at our monthly staff meetings, we always reward one employee, with a bonus or gift, based on how well they upheld the core values the month before. I always tell him or her, "You wear your T.I.E.S. well."

I want to challenge you to instill core values for your team, your church, your company, or your organization. Use ours for inspiration but most importantly, select ones that reflect what you stand for. Think about the environment and culture you want and establish the core values necessary to achieve the vision and mission. Below are some examples of core values, though this is certainly not an exhaustive list:

- Reliable
- Committed
- Consistent
- Efficient
- Creative
- Fun-loving

- Motivated
- Optimistic
- Passionate
- Courageous
- Respected
- Nurturing
- Dependable
- Loyal
- Open-minded
- Honest
- Innovative
- Humorous
- Adventurous
- Positive
- Inspiring
- Respectful
- Athletic
- Fit
- Educated
- Loving

Recently, *YFS Magazine* listed the core values of fifteen winning companies. Here are four of the mentioned organizations and what standards they follow. Use their core values for inspiration as you create your own.

Zappos:
1. Deliver WOW Through Service
2. Embrace and Drive Change
3. Create Fun and a Little Weirdness
4. Be Adventurous, Creative and Open-Minded
5. Pursue Growth and Learning
6. Build Open and Honest Relationships with
7. Communication
8. Build a Positive Team and Family Spirit
9. Do More with Less
10. Be Passionate and Determined
11. Be Humble

Teach For America:
1. Transformational Change
2. Leadership
3. Team
4. Diversity
5. Respect and Humility

Barnes & Noble Booksellers:
1. Customer Service
2. Quality
3. Empathy

4. Respect
5. Integrity
6. Responsibility
7. Teamwork

American Express:
1. Customer Commitment
2. Quality
3. Integrity
4. Teamwork
5. Respect for People
6. Good Citizenship
7. A Will to Win
8. Personal Accountability

Core values establish expectations you deem important. If you do not set any standards, you cannot hold anyone accountable. Create a culture in your team where the criteria for successful performance is expected and celebrated!

Warning: once you make your values public, people expect you to uphold them.

We need to set core values with our team!

Chapter Seven

7

Set Yearly Goals

If you aim at nothing, you'll hit it every time.

Imagine that it's New Year's Eve. You're wearing a festive party hat and "Aude Lange Sine" is playing in the background. As you reflect over the past twelve months with a smile from ear to ear, you cheerfully declare, "This has been the most amazing year of my life!"

What would need to happen for you to say that? The answer to that question is how you determine your goals.

Define a Successful Year

> Where there are no goals, neither will there be significant accomplishments; there will only be existence.
>
> — Anonymous

Your goals are targets. You need to determine the bulls-eye(s) to hit this year in order to feel that it was a successful one. You must define what a successful year looks like *to you* before you begin taking steps toward it.

This could mean:
- You pay off your school loans of $16,437.08.
- You complete your Master's Degree.
- Your church attendance grows by 20%.
- Your sales increase by 20%.
- Your TV viewership expands into five new territories.
- You launch a new division.
- You publish your first book.
- Your team hits another record.

Setting goals means deciding what you want, planning how to get it, and then going after it! God wants you to have goals and intermediate objectives that you strive toward each year. It's one thing to have a big dream, but it's vital that you have smaller dreams (goals) that you can focus on now.

> One thing I do, forgetting the things which are behind, and stretching forward to the things which are before, I press on toward the goal unto the prize of the high calling of God in Christ Jesus.
> —Philippians 3:13-14 NIV

Statistics show that people who make New Year's Resolutions are ten times more likely to attain their goals than people who don't make resolutions. Bottom line: setting goals increases your opportunity for success.

Dr. David Kohl, a professor at Virginia Tech University, conducted research on successful people and goal setting. In this study, he discovered that people who set goals for their life earn "nine times as much" as those who don't.[6]

Setting goals is a lot like playing darts:

- All you need to play is: (1) a set of three darts (2) a dartboard (3) a wall to hang it on.

6 Daniel Wong, Reflections of a compulsive goal-setter, The Duke Chronicle, April 26, 2011, (http://www.dukechronicle.com/articles/2011/04/06/reflections-compulsive-goal-setter).

- You can play alone or with others.
- With practice and skill, you can improve.
- Age and gender do not matter (whether you're 10 or 80, male or female, you can play).
- It doesn't take a lot of money to play.
- You can play at various levels (as a beginner, at home, or with a group in a public setting).
- It's a huge morale booster. It doesn't take long for people to bond and become a team when playing this game together.

Why all the useless facts about a game you may or may not even care about? Because having a target for your life, business, organization, or ministry is vital to your success. Without a target, there's nowhere to aim.

In my years as a CEO of an international organization, I believe one of the strengths that God has given me is defining our target for each endeavor and putting all our efforts into hitting it time after time.

In his classic book, *Think & Grow Rich,* Napoleon Hill analyzed several thousand men and women, of which 98 percent were categorized as "failures." He determined, "Lack of a well-defined purpose in life" was the pitfall. In fact, 98 out of the 100 people analyzed had *no aim*. Hill concluded, "There is no hope of success for the person who does not have a definite goal at which to aim."

Vision First – Ideas Second

Michael Hyatt's rise in Thomas Nelson, the publishing company is a true testament of the power of vision. When he came on board, Michael inherited a particular division that was in terrible shape. It was the least profitable with no growth for three years, and everyone who worked there was exhausted and void of morale.

Contrary to what most executives would do, Michael's first step wasn't to strategize ways to turn the division around. Through his years of experience, he discovered that focusing on the "how" rather than the "what" blocks people from thinking big. Michael knew he needed a clear vision, a target. He says in his article, *Why Vision is More Important than Strategy*, "If you have a clear vision, you will eventually attract the right strategy. If you don't have a clear vision, no strategy will save you."

Vision first, ideas second.

What did Mike do? He developed a target at which to aim. He went away on a private retreat to spend time discovering his "dart board." He wasn't concerned with strategy; his only concern was developing a vision for what he wanted the company to look like in three years. He materialized that vision into a statement: "Nelson Books is the world's largest, most respected provider of inspirational books." He then listed the specifics of what he foresaw in the future. These included the following (as well as others relating to profitability, rapid growth, employee bonuses, and a reputation for being the most sought-after publishing company):

- We have ten franchise authors whose new books sell at least 100,000 copies in the first 12 months.
- We are publishing 60 new titles a year.
- The top agents routinely bring us their best authors and proposals because of our reputation for success.
- We place at least four books a year on the *New York Times* bestsellers list.[7]

7 Michael Hyatt, Why Vision is More Important Than Strategy, January 23, 2012, (http://michael-hyatt.com/why-vision-is-more-important-than-strategy.html).

Mike personally read these statements every day. He asked God for guidance. He dreamed about them. He prayed over every part. They were constantly before his eyes. As he did these things first, strategies began to naturally emerge.

Mike's dream was to turn the division around within three years. However, he had exceeded almost every aspect of his vision in a mere eighteen months. Not long after, Mike was promoted from the head of his division to CEO of the entire Thomas Nelson organization.

> Setting goals is the first step in turning the invisible into the visible.
> —Tony Robbins

Dream of the end result. Get focused. What is your target? Be clear on where you need to aim. Do not allow your mind to become consumed with *how* you are going to achieve. You must know where you want to go before you start taking steps to get there.

Write Them Down

In Chapter 2, I mentioned Napoleon Hill interviewing five hundred of the wealthiest people in the world. If you recall, every single person practiced the same success principle—they each had clearly-defined, written goals.

> You are never too old to set another goal
> or to dream a new dream.
> —C.S. Lewis

Be certain of this, it is not enough to keep your dreams in your head. You must take the time to put your goals in writing. I can't stress this enough.

I've heard stories about how Lou Holtz, the legendary coach of Notre Dame, practiced writing his dreams and goals with much success. In 1966, out of a job and with his pregnant wife at home, Lou had no idea what he was going to do with his life. The solution came when his wife bought him a book on the power of thinking big. As Lou read this eye-opening path to a new life, he was encouraged to put in writing every single thing he wanted to accomplish before he died.

121

Holtz reportedly sat at the kitchen table that night and let his imagination run wild. He ended up listing 107 life goals, including:

- Have dinner at the White House
- Coach at Notre Dame
- Lead my team to a national championship
- Appear on the *Tonight Show*
- Meet the pope
- Shoot a whole-in-one in golf

To date, Lou has achieved 102 of the 107 things on his list! You must define success in writing before you try to achieve it.

Years ago, Bruce Jenner, Olympic gold medalist in the decathlon, met with a room full of Olympic hopefuls and asked how many of them had their dreams and goals written down somewhere. Every single hand in the place went up (which speaks volumes). He also asked the athletes if they had their written dreams and goals with them at that moment. One hand went up: Dan O'Brien's. O'Brien went on to win a 1996 Olympic Gold Medal in Atlanta, Georgia.

Each year, I practice the same exercise I started this chapter with: by imagining it is the last day

The importance of writing your goals daily & carrying them with you!

of the year and looking back at the previous twelve months with joyful excitement over the accomplishments God enabled us to achieve. I say to my family and colleagues, "This has been the most amazing year of my life!" Then I very simply ask myself what needs to happen for me to make a statement that bold. And I begin writing.

I want you to do the same. You need a target. Your family needs a target. Your team needs a target. Your staff, your colleagues, your children, and your business partners need to know where to aim this year.

You Become What You Behold

Whatever your bulls-eye is for the year, it must be in sight. I used to write down my New Year's resolutions on January 1 and put them in my nightstand, never to be reviewed again.

Did I achieve them? Ha! I could never even remember what I wrote, nor where I placed them. Since I began practicing the art of setting goals and keeping them clearly before my eyes, I now see results. I continually achieve my goals year after year.

The Word of God offers us a powerful principle—You become what you behold. This is the law of vision.

> But we all, with unveiled face, beholding as in a mirror the glory of the Lord, are being transformed into the same image from glory to glory, just as from the Lord, the Spirit.
>
> —2 Corinthians 3:18 NASB

Notice this scripture says that we are "transformed into the same image." The same image as what? What you are beholding? Joshua 1:8 tells us to behold the Word of God. Why? Because what you behold, you become.

To behold something doesn't mean to glance at it every once in a while. Synonyms of behold include the following: see, view, consider, study, watch, regard, observe, perceive, gaze, and contemplate. What are you looking at? What are you seeing? You need to see images of what your life can look like. Stop looking at reality and thinking this is as good as it gets. You have to *see* something before you can *have* something.

In Dodie Osteen's book, *Healed of Cancer*, she describes how her body began deteriorating with her disease. When she looked in the mirror, she vividly saw a frail, sick, weak body. She knew she had to change what she saw if she was going to claim victory over cancer.

Dodie went through all her family photo albums and found pictures of when she was in perfect health, alive and full of energy. She hung those pictures up all over the house, on the refrigerator, the bathroom mirror, in picture frames. Dodie needed to see herself healed and alive. She surrounded herself with what "could be" not what "was." That's vision. That's faith. Today, she once again resembles that picture of perfect health.

If you want to provide even more inspiration to your life, your team, and your family, design a vision board for everyone to see. When you add pictures to your goals, it causes the vision to become more real and seem more attainable. The first time you *behold* the images you desire, you may laugh or snicker at the humorous size of your goal; however, the more you stare at the vision, the more real it appears.

Follow these quick steps to creating a vision board for your yearly goals. You can be as creative or as simple as you want, but use images of your goals to stay focused on where you want to go. This exercise will take your goal-setting discipline to a whole new level.

5 Steps to Creating a Vision Board

Step 1: Think, pray, and listen.

What's on your mind? What goal is God telling you to get serious about pursuing? Do you need to cut your expenditures by a considerable amount, increase production, or simply meet on a consistent basis with your team? Whatever it is, write it down.

Step 2: Purchase the backdrop for your vision board.

You can use a simple poster board, corkboard, or bulletin board, or you can jazz it up like I did by framing a corkboard with a funky frame. You can even use a notebook or journal, if you prefer.

Step 3: Find pictures to match your goals.
Because our minds think in pictures not words, I find it very helpful to cut out images that depict my dreams. Browse through magazines, catalogs, and brochures and tear out images that match your goals for your team or organization. You can even use printable online photos. Glue or pin all your pictures to the board. Have fun with this step! I have a photo on my vision board of thousands of women at a convention center with the word "Icing" on the backdrop of the stage.

Step 4: Be specific.
Habakkuk 2:2 encourages us to write the vision and make it plain. If you want to pay off your department's debt, write the dollar amount of the debt with the words "paid in full" over it. Be specific. Vague goals produce vague results.

Step 5: Keep it in sight.
The Contemporary English Version translates Habakkuk 2:2 this way: "I will give you my message in the form of a vision. Write it clearly enough to be read at a glance." Hang your vision board in a place where you will look at it often.

Out of sight is out of mind. The key is to look at it as much as possible. This way, you will be constantly aware of where your life is headed.

If you want to see your dreams and your goals unfold before your eyes, don't underestimate the power of writing your yearly goals *and* keeping them before your eyes.

Chapter Eight

8
Know the Facts

People are destroyed for a lack of
knowledge.
—Hosea 4:6

Excellent leaders make decisions based on facts.
The more you know, the better equipped you are to
lead your team to success. The truth is, you cannot
make good decisions with poor information.

You cannot separate leadership from decision-
making. Making sound decisions is a skill that
must be developed in order to be an effective
leader. Your team will rise or fall based on that
ability.

In my early days of leadership, I tried my best to
obtain as much information as I could with regard
to each department of the organization. However,
the information I received was extremely vague.

For instance, I would ask, "How many books
sold at the convention last week?"

"Quite a few," the department head would reply.

"Is that a lot?" I would ask, uncertain of the success from their response.

"It's above average. Not too many, but a fair amount."

What does any of that mean? Does "quite a few" and "above average" mean we sold two hundred books, two thousand books, or ten thousand books? Does anyone even know how many books were sold last year to compare the data to?

My staff and I can laugh about it now but the feedback was confusing, nonspecific, and ill prepared. You can't improve what you can't measure, and you can't measure without good data. ee. 9 CORE STEPS IN OUR BUSINESS.

As a leader, you are responsible for making major decisions, and if you are not receiving the accurate information that you need, your choices could lead to disaster.

At the CEO workshop I attended early on, Dr. Dean Radtke shared that CEOs are most often fired for the following reasons:

- 31% poor management
- 28% ignored the customer base
- 27% tolerated poor performance
- 23% failed to recognize reality

I wonder how many of those statistics relate directly to the CEO not having a complete picture of their organization, staff, core values, policies, financial picture, and so on. If the information you need is not just handed to you, go and find it. Part of being a leader is acquiring the knowledge you need to make informed decisions. Taking initiative will show your team that you are serious and dedicated to the task at hand and will encourage them to step up their game as well.

Change Only Comes with Facts

Facing reality often causes a push for change. You need to know exactly what is going on in your business, church, team, or company. It is imperative that you embark on a fact-finding mission.

- Is your church growing or not? If so, by how many members compared to last year?
- Are you spending more money than you're earning? How much? Where do you need to cut back?
- Is your product selling or sitting on a shelf? What is your inventory?
- Are people responding to your message or not? How can you determine response? Purchases? Phone calls? Mail orders?
- Are you losing customers faster than you gain them? How many?
- Are people viewing your podcasts or not? How many subscribers do you have compared to last year?
- Is your social media account growing? If so, how many new followers since last month?

The most successful organizations make decisions based on facts and data-driven information. No matter how small or how large your organization, church, ministry, or team, you will fail or succeed based on the quality of your decision-making.

You need to know, by the facts presented to you, which area of your organization needs the greatest amount of change. When you discover what that is, the majority of your time, energy, and resources need to be spent fixing the problems. You must review every aspect of your business to know where you are healthy as an organization and where you suffer weakness.

Knowing the facts could mean learning about the following specifics:

Finances:
- Income vs. budget (monthly)
- Expenses vs. budget (monthly)
- Month-to-date income
- Yearly comparison (month-to-month)
- Accounts payable
- Savings
- Investment account

Event (or church) Attendance:
- Meeting attendance (compare weekly, monthly, annually)
- First-time attendees

Ministry:
- Salvations, rededications
- New members
- Assimilation of new members

- Small groups (attendance)

Media:

- Books sold
- TV response (ROI)
- Social media subscriptions, followers, reposts

Demographics of your market:

- Age
- Location
- Gender
- Average income
- Educational background

How can you plan for growth if you are unclear about your present state? If you are running a church and your "first-time visitors" record has increased but your overall weekly attendance has remained the same as last year, then you are, in fact, losing people. You need to know the facts in order to make wise decisions going forward. If people are leaving your church, then you need to figure out how to close the back door.

I remember celebrating when we gained nearly 10,000 new contacts in our organization's database; however, by obtaining more facts, we discovered an overall loss of 11,000 people from our database. Put the party hats, the whistles, and the cake aside—new information changes the facts.

Let's say that you are preparing to print a new book. Your team brings options for printing costs, which reveal that the more you order, the more money you save per unit. Sounds great!

Proposal:
- Purchase 1,000 books at $5.00 per unit = $5,000
- Purchase 5,000 books at $3.50 per unit = $17,500
- Purchase 10,000 books at $2.00 per unit = $20,000

Faced with those numbers (and those facts alone), you conclude that for only $2,500 more, you could purchase another 5,000 books! No brainer, right? However, what you don't realize is that, on average, you sell approximately 1,000 books per year. Therefore, it could take nearly ten years to sell 10,000 books. That results in ten years of inventory taking up warehouse space, book quality deteriorating in boxes, and profits from the book materializing over a five to ten-year time span.

> My faith works on facts—not on
> approximates.
>
> —Jerry Savelle

My dad always warned me never to come to him with approximates or guesses. In other words, don't say that you need approximately $7,000 for a project if it really costs $7,853.16. Know all the facts and make decisions based on accurate information and train your team to do the same.

Even coaches make decisions based on facts. The Los Angeles Lakers know to have Kobe Bryant take the final shot when the team is behind. The facts show his career field goal percentage of 45.4 percent gives the team the best chance of winning.[8]

Many leaders make decisions based on gut feelings or the urgency of the moment, but it is always better to base decisions on facts. Train your team to obtain accurate information. Record everything. It's better to have too much information than not enough. Outstanding leaders are rarely <u>caught off guard.</u>

8 Leslie Stevens-Huffman, "How to use big data to make better business decisions," Smart Business Network, Inc. (2014): accessed June 23, 2014, http://www.sbnonline.com/component/k2/13-national-editions/25626#.U6g-ohbi71o

Chapter Nine

9

Establish a Financial Plan

The wise have wealth and luxury but
fools spend whatever they get.
                              – Proverbs 21:20

In the beginning days of leading our organization
as CEO, I realized we were spending more than
we were earning. I had to immediately determine
the financial targets of our organization or watch
us head into severe disaster. My team and I began
to define what "financial health" looks like in our
company.

Building a strong foundation and having a
clear vision of healthy financial management will
significantly impact you and your organization.
I am not recommending that you know your
financial position; I'm saying it is an absolute
necessity. It's critical to your success. And it
should be your first priority.

Financial health is the state of your financial situation. It can include the amount of savings your company has, the amount you are putting away for investments, and how much you are spending on fixed expenses. Each situation is different, so you must define what financial health means for you and your business.

Understanding the health of your company's finances is more than just logging in to your bank account and glancing at your balances. You need to have a broad picture of what is going on. You must have vision of where you want to be financially over the next twelve months, the next five years, and even ten years from now.

As the old saying goes, "Cash is king." A healthy organization will work diligently to ensure that the money coming in exceeds the funds flowing out. However, it has been my experience, in working with numerous organizations and learning about their financial patterns, that many find themselves in financial jeopardy when the unexpected occurs because they lack financial vision.

In one year alone, our organization footed the bill for FIVE funerals! We were grateful for the financial ability to help the families in need, but the lack of financial planning of these families was evident. These weren't folks living in poverty or needy families receiving government aid. Unfortunately, these were leaders and owners of organizations who spent everything they earned and did little to prepare for their financial future.

Recently, I heard that a renowned minister built a 25-million-dollar facility on pledges from his church members. He was given a commitment of 27 million dollars but only received 2 million. Not long after, he had a heart attack and suffered from a stroke. Now what?

Proverbs 29:18 is just as applicable to your financial vision as it is to any dream you have: If you do not have a vision for your finances personally and for your business, they will perish.

Read these startling facts of the "average" person from *The Automatic Millionaire*:

- 43.7 million households in the U.S. have less than $1,000 in savings account
- Nearly 60 million (1 in 5) have nothing in the bank.
- Wall Street Journal reports 70% of Americans

live paycheck to paycheck
- Average American currently owes more than $8,400 in credit card debt.
- 80% of graduating college seniors have credit-card debt (before they even have a job!)
- 19% of the people who filed bankruptcy last year were college students![9]

> The average American is busy buying things he doesn't want with money he doesn't have to impress people he doesn't like.
>
> —O. Donald Olson

Remember, thinking precedes achievement. Do you have a clear financial vision? Give these questions some thought:

- How much money do you want to save over the next 12 months? What is that exact number?
- How much debt do you have? Have you added it all up together? Are you afraid to know?
- How much of your debt do you want paid off in one year?

9 David Bach, The Automatic Millionaire (Broadway Books, 2005).

- How much does it cost to finance your dreams and goals? Have you done the math? Do you know how much money it will take to broadcast on that TV network? Or build that new building? Or purchase the new company car? Or hire more staff? Or start your retirement fund?

Determine Change in Your Finances

> The habits you currently have are only good enough to get you what you've currently got. If you want different results, change your habits.
> —Bill Chandler

I firmly believe that once the vision is clear, the provision is near. God wants "above all things that you prosper and be in health even as your soul prospers" (3 John 2). He wants you to be blessed so you can be a blessing! It is easy to become distracted when your financial targets are not clear. For this reason, I have provided a six-step guide toward financial security in your personal and business life.

1. Educate yourself and your team about money.

There is no shortage of statistics revealing the downside of winning the lottery. Whether it is 70% or 1 in 3 winners who lose it all, the numbers are alarming. The National Endowment for Financial Education conducted research estimating that 70% of people suddenly receiving large sums of money will lose it within a few years. If your life is to be changed for the better by money, you must change the way you think about money.

Hosea 4:6 says, "My people are destroyed for a lack of knowledge." One translation says we are "doomed" for a lack of knowledge. Doomed means we are destined to fail or marked by an ill-fated future. Ouch! Simply not knowing what to do with your money could be your greatest downfall.

So, what is the solution? As Dave Ramsey puts it, "If you want to be skinny, study skinny people. If you want to be wealthy, study wealthy people. If you want to be successful, study successful people."[10] We have to choose to study, to absorb, and become educated about our finances.

---

10 Dave Ramsey, Total Money Makeover (Thomas Nelson, 2013).

One of my team's reading assignments was the bestselling book *Rich Dad, Poor Dad* by Robert Kyosaki. I was struck by the story of a wealthy woman whose home was burglarized. The thieves stole typical valuables around the house like jewelry and electronics, but they left what she considered most valuable—her books. These books are what educated this woman and taught her how to become wealthy. The author explains the importance of these books to the character.

Too many people are focused too much on money and not their greatest wealth, which is their education. If people are prepared to be flexible, keep an open mind and learn, they will grow richer and richer through the changes. If they think money will solve the problems, I am afraid those people will have a rough ride. Intelligence solves problems and produces money. Money without financial intelligence is money soon gone.

When my team truly understood that we were operating at a deficit each month and the savings account was dwindling fast, I gave a directive: no new expenses. It was something each of us had to abide by, no matter what. When an opportunity arose that seemed promising, NO NEW EXPENSES! When the computer broke down, NO NEW EXPENSES! When a TV time slot was offered to us at rock bottom prices, NO NEW EXPENSES! When the company car we needed was at an all-time low price, NO NEW EXPENSES! It was hard, to say the least, but we were determined to get ahead financially and stop treating God's resources with disrespect.

If we wastefully spend everything we get, then why would God bless us with more? In many cases, more money will not solve our problems. The problem may actually increase, as people tend to spend more as they earn more.

My team and I were determined to educate ourselves in the area of finances. You can spend all evening watching television (according to The Nielson Co., most Americans watch four hours per day), or you can take twenty minutes and read a good book, such as *The Total Money Makeover* by Dave Ramsey. Invest in yourself. Invest in change. Invest in your future. Your new mindset will progressively lead you toward the attainment of the financial future you desire.

If you want next year to be different than this year, do something different. Don't keep saying: "Someday we're going to have more savings in our church." or "Someday I'm going to get serious about getting out of debt." Someday is not a day of the week. You waste time stuck in wishful thinking instead of taking action. Debt is piling up. Money is being spent. Opportunities are being missed. Dreams are going unfulfilled. Get educated. Start learning. And start working toward your financial vision.

2. Define your financial targets.

Entrepreneur.com reported that a staggering "84% of respondents to a New Year's Resolution Survey from Allianz Life Insurance said that financial planning was not among their resolutions at all…" What was preventing them from planning? "Well, 30% said they don't believe they make enough money to 'worry' about financial planning."[11]

In Chapter 7, we discussed the importance of

---

11 Ric Edelman, 8 Financial Planning Tips to Keep in mind this Year, Entrepreneur, Feb. 2, 2014, (http://www.entrepreneur.com/article/231069).

having a target. You must identify your financial target so you know where to aim. I recommend the 80/10/10 approach.

- Live on 80%.
- Tithe 10%.
- Save 10%.

Live on 80%
Create a budget (which I will discuss in my next point) based on 80 percent of your company's total monthly income. Make adjustments to live within this percentage. You may not be able to do this immediately, but make it a goal.

Tithe 10%
Tithing 10 percent of your income from your company, organization, or church is how you honor God with your finances. My dad says that tithing is not a *debt* that we owe but a *seed* that we sow. According to Malachi 3:10, the tithe belongs to God. You really haven't even touched your money when you tithe. You're simply giving God what already belongs to Him.

I believe with all my heart that when God

finds someone He can trust with money, He gives them more! It just makes sense. Jack Canfield says prosperity is a guarantee when we're tithing ten percent of our income, and I couldn't agree more.

You have to get to a place spiritually where you view the tithe as untouchable. I know from experience (and from the testimonies of thousands of other people) that your money will go much further living on ninety percent and tithing ten percent than trying to keep it all for yourself.

> Remember the Lord your God, for it is
> He who gives you the ability to produce
> wealth.
> —Deuteronomy 8:18 NIV

Save 10%
You know what will happen if you spend everything you make? You'll have nothing. If you keep this up over the next five years, what will you have? Nothing. If something tragic happened to your company or the economy took a major turn for the worse, what would you have stored up? Nothing?

Start wherever you are. And don't view something small as nothing at all. Saving $100 a week for one year will produce $5,200. Keep that in mind each day and see how much you can save.

Do you know what ten percent of your monthly income is? Set a goal to tithe and to save that percentage every month. Initially, you may not be able to start saving ten percent. When our organization began implementing financial targets, we were using *every* dollar that came in just to make ends meet. I was determined to start somewhere. Remember, it is important that you never view small progress as no progress. Change adds up little by little.

I went to our Chief Financial Officer and said we were going to put a demand on our faith, starting with one percent. We began saving one percent every month. Then we increased to three percent. As we could, we saved more each month until we reached our saving's goal of depositing ten percent of our monthly revenue into our savings account.

Start saving no matter where you are financially. You will be amazed at how quickly it accumulates.

3. Establish a budget.

> We can tell our values by looking at our checkbook stubs.
> —Gloria Steinem

Some people view budgeting the same way they view dieting: going without. While challenging at first, it does not have to be an unpleasant experience. If you develop a positive mindset and keep it as simple as possible, establishing a realistic budget will set you up for an incredible financial future.

If I were to log into your company's bank account, what would it reveal about your financial priorities? How is your money being spent? Are your daily donuts and pastries for the staff really a priority? Are the company cell phones a necessity or a luxury? When we had to establish financial health in our organization, I had to pull out the magnifying glass out and look at every single expense.

Here are some questions to ask yourself as you think about creating a budget, whether for personal or business use:

Do you know your monthly income?
Once you have established your priorities and goals (80/10/10) you need to establish how much money comes in each month. You should know what your average monthly income is. You should be able to identify trends in your monthly income over the course of a year. When you are familiar with the trends, you don't get stressed out or concerned when income is lower one month over the previous month. You prepare for it.

Do you know your monthly expenditures?
You should be able to look at all of your monthly expense statements and know exactly how much you're spending. You need to be knowledgeable of your fixed expenses (rent, salaries, electricity, etc.). How much of your revenue is used to pay overhead costs?

Do you know where your money is going?
The key to making ends meet is keeping better track of your spending. "The best laid plans are often ruined by impetuous spending and undisciplined decisions," said David Francis.

Jeremy Vohwinkle, a chartered retirement planning counselor, suggests:

> The best place to start is to take inventory of where your money goes. A lot of people have a rough idea of where they spend, but take a month or two to see where the money's going and you'll be really shocked. You find places that you can cut back.

You should be able to look at your monthly budget and know exactly where money is being spent.

> Most of us waste a lot of what we earn on "small things"… the so-called small things on which we waste money every day can add up in a hurry to life-changing amounts that ultimately can cost us our freedom.
>
> —David Bach

It can be startling to learn how much money we spend on little things (lattes, magazines, eating out) because they appear so insignificant. However, day-by-day these little expenditures can drain our bank accounts and consume any plan of savings whatsoever.

David Bach, financial author and founder of Finishrich.com, is known for an eye-opening illustration that shows how much money we waste. He calls it the "Latte Factor." (For me, it's the Burrito Factor. I love my burritos! But thanks to him, I don't buy them as much as I used to.)

I like what *People Magazine* said when they wrote a story about this principle—"A latte spurned is a fortune earned."

Here's the example:

- A latte a day=$3.50
- A latte a day/month=$105.00
- A latte a day/year=$1,260.00
- A latte a day/decade=$12,600.00

Bach was teaching college students this powerful lesson on trivial spending when he added a daily muffin (another $3.50) to the illustration. Seven dollars doesn't seem like much to spend each day on breakfast, does it? Well, this monthly expenditure equals approximately $150!

To top it all off, Bach suggested that investing this amount of money every month and earning a 10 percent annual return would, over the course of forty years, produce approximately $948,611. That's nearly one million dollars from simply avoiding the coffee and cake. Incredible!

Making a few sacrifices is part of getting ahead financially and managing expenses. However, if you put too many restrictions on yourself, you'll be less likely to stick with them for a long period of time. You may need to eliminate four "latte's a day" for the week rather than eliminating them altogether. Don't set yourself up for failure.

4. Become Debt-Free

> Debt is the result of overspending and
> under-saving.
> —Dave Ramsey

You could be praying for a miracle to erase all your debt when God is simply saying, "Stop spending so much!" Debt is bondage. It's one of the top stress-producers in the world, and it will keep you from pursuing and achieving your dreams.

A survey from the Forbes 400 (a list of the richest 400 people in America) found that 75% of those on the list said the best way to build wealth is to become and remain debt-free. These wealthy people live on less than what they earn and spend only when they have cash to pay. They don't charge everything like so many of us do.

I only know how to teach from experience. I'm only telling you to do what God instructed me to do as I began educating myself in financial management. My team and I made a quality decision to be good stewards with the money God had entrusted us with. God wants you to be blessed and owe a debt to no man but to love him!

When you identify average monthly income for your personal life and/or organization, you have a clear number that you need to work around. Managing your money no longer becomes guesswork. This is what you have to work with.

You need to make the quality decision to live a debt-free life. It is possible. Obtaining a clear picture of your debt is the first step. Add it all up—every single bill. Get that number clear in your head and on paper. Print out a photo of a pile of money with the number of your debt boldly

[handwritten margin note: Visualize paying off your debt.]

156

typed. Keep that photo in sight at all times.

Many financial experts recommend paying off debts one at a time beginning with the smallest you have. Dave Ramsey has coined this concept the "debt snowball method." Pay the minimum on your other debts, but focus entirely on getting that lowest bill paid off. The psychological boost will inspire you to keep going until all debts are paid.

Paying OF debt "snow-ball" Method.

Someone once said, "You don't have to be great to get started but you have to get started to be great." Start where you are so that you will be one step closer to your financial dreams by this time next year.

If you are getting overwhelmed with late notices on past due accounts and phone calls from vendors and bill collectors, I recommend that you stop ignoring the calls, the letters, and the appointments. Make the effort to reach out to the creditors. Doing so speaks volumes of your character and your willingness to rectify the situation. Try to negotiate with the original creditor and work out a reasonable payment arrangement.

Simply pretending the debt isn't there or that it will magically go away could damage your credit report and your reputation. Ignoring phone calls due to embarrassment only makes the creditor angry and more frustrated with you.

I recommend three A's: (1) Apologize to the creditor. Go the extra mile to send an apology note or gift in the mail to them or a simple phone call made from you. (2) Arrange a payment plan based on what you can realistically afford and pay consistently. (3) Ask what they would be willing to negotiate or settle on. You have not because you ask not. (My co-worker had a loan reduced from $23,000 to $10,000 all because he asked!)

5. Save – Save – Save

Creating easy access to your funds can be a very tempting decision when it comes to saving money. I highly recommend setting up a plan where money is not easy to attain such as an automatic transfer from your general account into your savings account or investment fund.

It is vital to have an emergency savings fund in your business and personal life to cover unexpected expenses. Ideally, your emergency fund should be about three to six months of your monthly expenses.

To get started, invest $1,000 immediately into this fund. Gradually, build this account by making it a priority. Add a portion of every incoming payment to it. Determine your savings goal by determining how long your business, your ministry, or your family could survive with a revenue shortage or even no income for a while.

If something happened and income was drastically cut, how long could the business survive? Could you make it six months with minimal revenue? Could you make it three months? Could you make it two weeks? Could you last until Friday? These are real questions you need to answer. This is exactly how our organization started saving until we reached our goal of having six months of our monthly expenses in our savings and investment accounts.

If your personal monthly expenses are $5,000, then multiply that by six months and set a financial target of $30,000 in your emergency savings account. This is what it means to live wisely. This is having a plan to succeed on purpose. This is what Proverbs defines as wise. Do this same exercise with your business expenses.

Consistency is the key to change. This will require you, the leader, to decide and communicate that saving money is not up for debate. It's not up for discussion. Determine you will put those finances aside in order to be wise stewards with the money that God gives your organization or business.

6. Invest in your dream.

I cannot leave out this vitally important step in securing your financial well-being. My Dad taught me this profound principle: You may not have what you *need* but you are never without the *seed* that will produce it. This unlocks the door to financial blessing. Anytime I have a dream or a goal that I want to pursue, I think to myself, *I need to sow a financial seed for it.*

God is seed-minded while we tend to be need-minded. When you are desperate for a financial turnaround in your life, that's when you need to sow a financial seed the most. Seed (money) represents future. It is what will soon come.

For example, a farmer realizes that his seed will not benefit him as long as it stays in the package. He must sow it. He also knows exactly for what he is sowing his seed. He doesn't toss it out into the wind and just wonder what will be produced. He is specific about what he plans to harvest. You shouldn't be any different. When you have a need (to get out of debt, to save $1,000, to pay off the company to print your book, to pay off your credit card bills), you should always sow a seed. When you are experiencing your greatest needs, sow your greatest seeds. No, this may not make sense with our natural minds, but this is a spiritual law that God put in place—and it works!

When Rodney and I were believing to move into our first home, we needed over $4,000 as a down payment. At that time in our lives we had $100 in our saving's account. We had a big need, so I knew it would require an even bigger seed.

What did we do? We gave the $100. That simple amount may not have been much to someone else, but it represented the best financial offering we had. It was *all* that we had. It was significant seed that resulted in our having the $4,000 to move into our new house on time.

The same thing happened with our second house. We needed $38,000 and had only $1,000 in savings. *When you're experiencing your greatest need, sow your greatest seed.* The greatest seed we had was $1,000. So, we gave it. After that, God brought us opportunities to make money, and we miraculously had the $38,000 needed to move in! When it looks like the most ridiculous thing to do, that's when you need to sow something significant.

Sow generously

> Whoever sows sparingly will also reap sparingly, and whoever sows generously will also reap generously.
> —2 Corinthians 9:6

We've taken this same action I'm talking about in our organization as well. Just recently in fact, we had need of a new office location. One of the very first steps we took was to give a sizable donation to an organization that had amazing favor with a building purchase. We do what we can physically, but in sowing financial seed, we also rely on God to do above and beyond that.

You might say, "Terri, I don't have much." Trust me on this one—the size of the seed isn't as important as the significance of the seed.

In 1 Kings, we read the story of the Prophet Elijah, who visited a widow and her son as they prepared to eat their last meal and die.

> Elijah said to her, "Don't worry about a thing. Go ahead and do what you've said. But first make a small biscuit for me and bring it back here. Then go ahead and make a meal from what's left for you and your son. This is the word of the GOD of Israel: 'The jar of flour will not run out and the bottle of oil will not become empty before GOD sends rain on the land and ends this drought.'"[12]

In other words, before you consume your last meal, give it. Don't hang on to it. Invest it. Sow it.

This widow was willing to give all that she had. It didn't matter that it was only a small biscuit. What mattered was her action. She did it. She gave God her best and, in return, God gave her and her child life. What are you willing to give for your dream? What is a significant seed you can sow for it? What kind of kingdom-of-God investment do you need to make?

12 1 Kings 17:13-14, THE MESSAGE BIBLE

> A man's harvest in life depends entirely
> upon the seeds that he sows.
> —Galatians 6:7 PHILLIPS

Any time you invest in your dream, your commitment level goes way up. It's a way of buying a stake in the game, which means investing something of value. John Maxwell says, "When you have a stake in the game, you no longer have an easy come, easy go attitude about it. You are invested in it."

> It is one of the beautiful compensations of
> this life that no man can sincerely try to
> help another without helping himself.
> —Ralph Waldo Emerson

Pray about what you need to give and where you need to give it. Then determine to obey what God is speaking to your heart. Delayed obedience is still disobedience. Partial obedience is still disobedience. When you obey God, you open the door for Him to begin moving in your life. You give yourself room for your financial dream to come to pass.

Chapter Ten

10
Stay Focused On Your Priorities

> Decide what your priorities are and how much time you'll spend on them. If you don't someone else will.
> —Harvey Mackay

A motivational speaker once said, "There are two things that are most difficult to get people to do: to think and to do things in order of importance." He expounded his point by saying that these two things are the difference between a professional and an amateur.

Evaluate Your Priorities

Since the responsibilities of a leader are enormous, you must decide what to do and what not to do. In many cases, this is easier said than done. In order to establish your major priorities, John Maxwell recommends that you answer the following three questions:

1. What is required of me?

In other words, what is expected of you that nobody else can do? Would failing to do this task(s) result in major negative outcomes for your business, organization, or ministry?

For me, message development is something only I can do (or I choose to do). I do not delegate my message preparation to anyone. Knowing that this is a high priority in my business, I must schedule this priority on my calendar.

2. What gives me the greatest return?

Are you working in your strength zone and receiving the greatest return on investment? My husband, Rodney, is an entrepreneur and a gifted salesman. He excels in conversation and pitching products and services, which makes him an asset to any company.

3. What is most rewarding?

What do you find fulfilling about what you do? You were designed to enjoy your life. Think about what you find most satisfying about your job.

When I came across these three questions, I asked my leadership team (and myself) to think about and answer them in explicit detail. We began to list every single duty/task we were responsible for at that time. The more we thought and wrote down, the more our lists seemed excessively lengthy and unrealistic. This explained why stress levels were at an all time high!

Once the list was compiled, I told everyone to circle tasks that only they could do. One by one we reviewed our lists and recognized a few assignments that could be delegated. Then we considered who was most capable to take on those particular responsibilities in the organization. And the delegation process began. (Side note: I recommend doing this exercise more than once. It is important to regularly re-evaluate priorities in your business, ministry, or organization.)

Most of us have a tendency to take on too many priorities. This puts us back where we started: stressed out, full of anxiety, and on the verge of burning out!

William H. Hinson explains how lion tamers use a whip, a pistol, and a four-legged stool to command the animals. Hinson stresses that the stool, a seemingly inferior defense, remains the most important tool of the trainer. Lion tamers always hold the stool by the seat and thrust the legs toward the face of the lion. This is an intentional tactic to force the lion to focus on all four legs of the stool at once. Doing this fragments the lion's attention. He becomes overwhelmed and therefore weak and tame.

If you are focused on too many priorities, you will become one fragmented mess, incapable of completing your purpose and carrying out your vision.

Are you too busy?

One day I purchased a book by Julie Morgenstern called, *Time Management from the Inside Out,* hoping it would inspire me to change. Ironically, I tucked away this gem in my nightstand for two months because I couldn't find time to learn how to manage my time! Then, out of sheer desperation, I finally planned time to read it. This book changed my life. I thank God that I finally educated myself in time management because it prepared me for what I'm doing today.

I want to show you how to view your time in a new way so you can accomplish all that God has for you without feeling constantly stressed, frazzled, or overwhelmed. In ten practical, life-changing solutions, you can find time to pursue what's most important to you in your business, organization, or ministry—not just the things you have to do, but also the God-callings He wants you to pursue.

> We don't have an eternity to realize our
> dreams, only the TIME we are here.
> —Susan Taylor

1. Identify your priorities.

We've talked about this already. Revisit the things you are choosing to focus on in your business, company, ministry, or organization. Write down the major responsibilities that only you can accomplish. Keep that list ever present before your eyes in order to stay focused on only those things. Delegate the rest.

2. Establish clear goals.

We've also talked about setting clear, not vague goals. If you are floundering around in your day-to-day life without any clear direction as to what needs to get done and by when, you are apt to forget important things or just never get them done. You must know what you want.

3. Schedule your priorities on your calendar.
One of the biggest questions we must ask ourselves when setting goals is *when will I do this?* You must schedule time on your daily planner to take action.

If one of your priorities is to finish your employee assessments this month, then you must schedule specific days to work on them. Write down *when* you will follow through.

4. Use a consistent planner.
You need one planner for everything. Schedule your work, your family time, your exercise, your social life—everything in this one planner. It may be an iPad, your phone, a pocket calendar, a day timer, or a wall calendar.

5. Recognize (and avoid) distractions.
Do you know that you can lose as much as two hours a day because of distractions? You can waste precious minutes, hours, and even days

on unnecessary emails, social media, phone calls, mindless chatter, online browsing, and so on. Think of how much you could get done if you had that time back!

When we are distracted, we are less focused on getting things done. Think about what you do on a regular basis that you can do without (like what I've mentioned above). Then eliminate them from your days and even your life.

> Most time is wasted in minutes, not hours. The average person diddles away enough minutes in ten years to have earned a college degree.
> —Dale Turner, *Seattle Times*

6. Honor your energy cycles.

Some people are more productive in the morning; others are night owls and therefore more efficient in the evening. We all have different times of the day in which we excel. I used to pray in the evening and would feel tired, rushed, and distracted. I finally realized I am most alert and ready to tackle tasks first thing in the morning. When I became aware of this, I began scheduling my most important to-dos (prayer time, exercise, and writing) in the morning. It's important to know when you are most energetic.

> Energy is power; it is what enables you to move toward your goals. Once you recognize and understand your natural energy sources and cycles, you can begin to manage them. Without being tuned in, you may be trying to tackle your most challenging activities when you're feeling sluggish and wasting your peak energy on less demanding tasks.[13]

7. Organize your workspace.

A disorganized environment will steal time and energy from your day. *The Wall Street Journal* reports that the average executive loses six weeks per year searching for missing information in messy desks and files. That breaks down to just one hour per day per person.

Clutter and disarray can block your success. The average office takes just three days to organize;

---

13 Julie Morgenstern, Time Management from the Inside Out (Henry Holt & Co. LLC, 2000).

the average room requires about one to two. It may be too overwhelming to organize your entire office, so start small. Start with your desk, your files, or the pile of paperwork that's been staring at you for weeks.

When you operate in an environment that is tidy and organized, you will feel better and have more clarity to focus on your priorities, your dreams, and your goals. Sometimes getting organized is the first step to focusing on your priorities!

8. Use a "Time Map."

People constantly ask me how I do so much and still find time to pray, exercise, enjoy my family, and work. To begin with, I learned how to use a "Time Map," a precious tool I learned about in *Time Management from the Inside Out*. It's been the greatest organizer of my time. I don't know what I would do without it! My Time Map has helped keep my days and my life in perspective and track how I spend the majority of my time.

A Time Map (an example of which you'll find on page 186 and a blank one for you to fill out on page 187) is simply a snapshot of your day that carves out specific times to do specific things. You build your Time Map according to your priorities.

All activities, to-do's, meetings, and appointments that you schedule on your Time Map must support these categories (or whatever ones you choose). This will help you prioritize your days and your life according to what's most important to you.

In her book, Morgenstern compares a packed schedule to a packed closet. Imagine an organized closet where every article of clothing and accessory has a designated spot. Your dresses have a place. Your handbags have a place. Your sweaters have a place. Your shoes have a place. If you buy a new pair of shoes, you know exactly where to put them on the shelf. There is no guesswork, no wasted time, no scrambling to find room. (Well, if you don't have the space for another pair of shoes, you will have to create more room or get rid of another pair so that your new purchase will fit. God forbid!)

Your Time Map works much the same way. If something comes up, like an appointment, a meeting, a seminar or a business lunch, you will be able to see right away whether you can easily fit it into your plans or whether you have to take time away from another activity to make room for it (if it is, in fact, more important).

I put everything in my Time Map—time spent writing books, taping TV broadcasts, traveling, conducting radio interviews, facilitating staff meetings, attending football games, going on dates with my husband, speaking at conferences, and so on. Scheduling everything I do keeps me focused, productive, and at peace.

To create your own time map, begin by writing down what you do (or need to do but don't) on a regular basis. Include appointments, activities, workshops, meetings, presentations, to-dos, and anything else that comes to mind. Map out these events in time increments. This tool will help you visualize how packed your day is, where you have extra time, and whether or not some activities are unnecessary and can be dropped. Take your time and tweak this Time Map as needed to prioritize what's most important and find a routine that works for you. Also, you may find it helpful to create a separate Time Map for different categories, like personal and work. (For more details, read *Time Management from the Inside Out*.)

9. Simplify your daily to-do's.

Most of us are completely unrealistic about what we can accomplish in a day. When we begin writing our unbelievable list of fifty-three things we need to do, it usually leaves us feeling frustrated and upset if at the end of the day we *only* checked off nineteen.

Calculating the amount of time my to-dos will take helps me create realistic lists for each day. This skill is one of the secrets the best time managers utilize to be more productive.

Many of us underestimate how long things like writing an article, meeting with an employee, preparing for meetings, or following up with a vendor usually take. If you don't allow appropriate time, you'll feel overwhelmed at the end of the day when you only accomplished one or two things.

You may think you only need:
- one hour to write an article;
- fifteen minutes to return two phone calls; or
- forty-five minutes to meet with a new employee.

But reality can look very different, especially if you're stuck on an idea, you can't rush the other person off the phone, or there's traffic. When you write down what you have to do in a day, I encourage you to allot enough time, even extra, just in case, to get them done. Give yourself two hours to write the article, a half hour to return phone calls, and an hour for the meeting.

Occasionally, we are shocked to see that a task we've been dreading because we thought it would be time-consuming took much less time than anticipated. Great! If you find yourself with extra time, use it to your advantage!

I encourage you to buy a timer or use one on your phone and begin timing the tasks you do every day to gain a realistic perspective.

Mary Kay Ashe, founder of Mary Kay Cosmetics, attributed her success to the fact that each day she made a list of the six most important goals to pursue. If she didn't complete all six, she carried them over to the next day. The point is that she was always focused on the *most important* things for the day.

Be realistic about your to-do list. Recognize what it is that could be holding you back and preventing you from feeling satisfied at the end of the day. Determine that you will conquer the clock and the calendar!

10. Plan each day the night before.

I never go to bed without planning my next day. In fact, when my daughter was four years old, I would tuck her in at night, pray with her, and then tell her the plan for the next day. One night when I returned to my bedroom, I heard Kassidi yelling over the intercom, "Mama! Mama!" I ran into her room to see what was so concerning. "Mama!" she cried. "You forgot to tell me the plan!"

(Okay, maybe I need a little spontaneity.)

A lack of planning is a time sucker. It's amazing how much you can accomplish in a day when you have a plan prepared ahead of time. When you have no idea what you need to do, time just seems to go by and you go to bed feeling unproductive.

John Maxwell plans his calendar over a month in advance. Even when he is taking time to relax outside of his normal routine, he has a plan for each day. Planning for the future is an important aspect of being successful in every part of your life.

> Anybody that's accomplished anything successful in life didn't get there by accident, they didn't get there haphazardly, they got there with a game plan.
>
> —Julie Morgenstern

What are the priorities you need to focus on in order to go to the next level in your business, ministry, or company?

Example: Write your book.

Perhaps God has been dealing with you about this for years but you just don't have TIME to write it. Remember, when you get to heaven God is going to hold you accountable for what he called you to. You must schedule time to write that book. It could be Tuesday and Thursday mornings from 9:00-11:00 a.m. Pencil it in.

Example: Learn a foreign language.

It could be that in order for you to get promoted, you need to learn Spanish or French but you just can't find time to study. Are you settling for a lower salary all because of your time management skills? Schedule your drive time to listen to audio lessons during your commute to school or work.

Example: Develop your mission statement.

What is one sentence that sums up your vision? When you determine this it accomplishes two things: (1) It helps you stay focused and not get distracted as you get busy. (2) It lets those who come along side to help you know what they're using their time and energy to achieve. Take time to think and write out a simple phrase that communicates your overall goal.

> What I do today is important because I am exchanging a day of my life for it.
> – Hugh Mulligan, *Associated Press*

Thee Priority!

Investing in your relationship with God should always be top priority! I cannot conclude these action steps without stressing the most important key to success: your relationship with God.

[handwritten margin note: Develop a mission statement, a reason "What" you're doing, what you're doing.]

181

Listening to motivational messages, developing a plan for personal growth, working with teams, knowing the facts are all vital in bringing your business or ministry's vision to pass, but nothing replaces your quality time with God.

Your consistent spiritual development is more valuable than anything else you could ever do in the pursuit of your dreams. Is it easy? No. It takes determination and discipline.

More than any other, this success habit will take you from where you are to where you want to be. Do something every day to communicate with God. Simply tell Him how much you need Him, respect Him, and love Him. He longs to hear from you just like an earthly mother or father enjoys a phone call or visit from their children (no matter what age).

Look for opportunities throughout your day to stay connected to God. Pray while you get your morning coffee. Hum a worship song when you refill your water bottle. Ask for guidance before meetings. Always be mindful that God is with you at all times.

→ Parallels message in church service 10.20.14

> ...for he that cometh to God must believe
> that he is, and that he is a rewarder of
> them that diligently seek him.
> —Hebrews 11:6

Matthew tells us to "seek *first* the kingdom of God and then all these other things will be added." (Matthew 6:33 [Emphasis added]) Your number one priority is your time spent with the Lord. As a leader, you are responsible for many things. People think it must be nice to be the boss, but to whom much is given, much is most definitely required. That's why it's important that you stay in the presence of God. You need to hear His voice.

People are looking to you for direction and leadership; and you need to stay dependent on hearing that still, small voice that tells you how and where to lead the organization. "Times of refreshing come in the presence of the Lord." (Acts 3:20) If you're stressed out, if you're full of anxiety, or if you're breathing hard because you've got all this pressure on you, the way to freedom is in the presence of the Lord.

If you have to, schedule your time with God on your calendar. Make this a habit, part of your daily routine. Whether it's five minutes, twelve minutes, twenty minutes, or two hours, do something to seek God each day.

> The only reason men fail is broken focus.
> —Unknown

I believe William Arthur Ward summed up the job description of an effective leader in this poem:

> You have to believe while others are doubting.
> Plan while others are playing.
> Study while others are sleeping.
> Decide while others are delaying.
> Prepare while others are daydreaming.
> Begin while others are procrastinating.
> Work while others are wishing.
> Save while others are wasting.
> Listen while others are talking.
> Smile while others are frowning.
> Commend while others are criticizing.
> And persist while others are quitting.

Being a leader is not easy; being an effective leader is even more challenging. However, if God has placed you in a position of leadership, then you are capable of becoming great. It takes a lot of time and hard work, but more effort makes things more valuable. An investment in your future will not go unreturned. Begin cultivating your leadership skills today and see the impact it will have on your business, organization, church, and family.

> Leaders are made, they are not born; and they are made just like anything else has ever been made in this country—by hard work.
> —Vince Lombardi

Sample Time Map

	Sun	Mon	Tue	Wed	Thur	Fri	Sat
5 a.m.		wake/prayer time	wake/ prayer time	wake/ prayer time	wake/ prayer time	wake/ prayer time	
6 a.m.		gym	gym	gym	gym	gym	
7 a.m.	wake	dress	dress	dress	dress	dress	
8 a.m.	dress	drive time/ audiobook	drive time/ audiobook	drive time/ audiobook	drive time/ audiobook	drive time/ audiobook	laundry/ cleaning
9 a.m.		office	office	office	office	office	laundry/ cleaning
10 a.m.	church	review goals		team meeting	prepare staff meeting	write book	
11 a.m.		email	podcast recording	team meeting		write book	
12 p.m.	family lunch	lunch	lunch	lunch with friends	lunch vacation plans	lunch	
1 p.m.					staff meeting		family time
2 p.m.	rest/ read	podcast notes					family time
3 p.m.			email	review proposals	email	email	family time
4 p.m.				email			
5 p.m.		drive time/ audiobook	drive time/ audiobook	drive time/ audiobook	drive time/ audiobook	drive time/ audiobook	
6 p.m.	pay bills	cook dinner	cook dinner	cook dinner	volleyball game		
7 p.m.					eat out	date night	
8 p.m.	prep week	read	pay bill	read			movie night
9 p.m.	read						
10 p.m.	plan week	sleep	sleep	sleep	sleep		
11 p.m.							

Time Map

	Sun	Mon	Tue	Wed	Thur	Fri	Sat
5 a.m.							
6 a.m.							
7 a.m.							
8 a.m.							
9 a.m.							
10 a.m.							
11 a.m.							
12 p.m.							
1 p.m.							
2 p.m.							
3 p.m.							
4 p.m.							
5 p.m.							
6 p.m.							
7 p.m.							
8 p.m.							
9 p.m.							
10 p.m.							
11 p.m.							

FURTHER RESOURCES FROM TERRI SAVELLE FOY

TERRI.COM

-Digital Magazine App
-Weekly Video Podcasts
-Product Specials
-Video/Audio Downloads
-Tour Dates
-And Much More...

PO Box 1959
Rockwall, Tx 75087

An easy, simple, and
effective way to help you
achieve your goals.

Terri Savelle Foy

For years, Terri Savelle Foy's life was average. She had no dreams to pursue. Each passing day was just a repeat of the day before. Finally, with a marriage in trouble and her life falling apart, Terri made a change. She began to pursue God like never before, develop a new routine and discovered the power of having a dream and purpose.

As Terri started to recognize her own dreams and goals, she simply wrote them down and reviewed them consistently. This written vision became a road map to drive her life. As a result, those dreams are now a reality.

Terri has become the CEO of an international Christian ministry. She is an author, a conference speaker, and a success coach to hundreds of thousands of people all over the world. Her best-selling books *Make Your Dreams Bigger than Your Memories*, and *Imagine Big* have helped people discover how to overcome the hurts of the past and see the possibilities of a limitless future. Her weekly podcast is a lifeline of hope and inspiration to people around the world.

Terri Savelle Foy is a cheerleader of dreams and is convinced that "if you can dream it, God can do it." She is known across the globe as a world-class motivator of hope and success through her transparent and humorous teaching style. Terri's unique ability to communicate success strategies in a simple and practical way has awakened the dreams of the young and old alike.

Terri shares from personal experience the biblical concepts of using the gift of the imagination to reach full potential in Jesus Christ. From stay-at-home moms to business executives, Terri consistently inspires others to go after their dreams. With step-by-step instruction and the inspiration to follow through, people are fueled with the passion to complete their life assignment down to the last detail (see John 17:4).

Terri and her husband, Rodney Foy, have been married since 1991, and are the parents of a beautiful redheaded daughter, Kassidi Cherie. They live near Dallas, Texas. For more information about Terri, go to www.terri.com.

Other books by Terri Savelle Foy

Make Your Dreams Bigger Than Your Memories

Untangle

Imagine Big

You're Valuable To God